The Jesus Digest

What You Never Knew About The Everyday Life of Jesus. Learn what It Was Like To Live When He Did.

By Dick Lattimer

"God has created me to do Him some definite service. He has committed some work to me which He has not committed to another. I have my mission. I may never know it in this life, but I shall be told it in the next. I am a link in a chain, a bond of connection between persons. He has not created me for naught. I shall do good...If I am in sickness, my sickness may serve Him; in perplexity, my perplexity may serve Him; if I am in sorrow, my sorrow may serve Him. He does nothing in vain. He knows what He is about. He may take away my friends. He may throw me among strangers. He may make me feel desolate, make my spirit sick, hide my future from me—still He knows what He is about."

Cardinal John Henry Newman
19th Century English Churchman

The Book That Answers These Questions...

- What was Jesus' real name?

- What was the house probably like that Jesus, Mary and Joseph lived in in Nazareth?

- Where was the town that Jesus and Joseph may have worked in?

- What was the Synagogue like that Jesus preached at in Capernaum?

- Has St. Peter's house that Jesus lived in in Capernaum ever been found?

- Who were the Apostles, what did they do, how long did they live, and how did they die?

- What did people eat in Galilee when Jesus lived?

- How did people like Jesus dress?

- What was the Sea of Galilee like, and what about the fishermen that lived on its shores and worked on its waters?

- What was the Jewish religion like in Jesus' days?

- As a good Jew, what prayers did Jesus say each day?

- What was the Temple like that Jesus worshiped in in Jerusalem?

...and much, much more!

Library of Congress Copyright Office Registration # TXu-1-041-279
International Standard Book Number 0-9611228-1-1

Printed in the U.S.A.

Front Cover: This is a Crown of Thorns made out of the Honey Locust Tree.
John The Baptist ate honey and locusts and baptized Jesus. If you would
like one of these life-sized Crown of Thorns for your home or church contact:
Crown of Thorns, P.O. Box 701, Wylie, TX 75098 or visit any fine Christian
bookstore or giftshop.

Permissions:

Permission from Richard A. Batey to use excerpts from his book "Jesus & the Forgotten City". Copyright © 1991 by Baker Book House Company.

Permission from Gerald F. McCauley to reprint portions of "The Mishnah: Oral Teachings of Judaism" by Eugene J. Lipman. The Viking Press. Copyright © 1970 by the B'nai B'rith Commission on Adult Jewish Education.

Permission from Baker Book House and from Dr. John McRay to use illustrations from his book "Archaeology & The New Testament". Copyright © 1991 by Baker Book House Company.

Permission from Mark Galli, Editor, to use "Did You Know" facts from Christianityonline.com/ChristianHistory and from Dr. John McKay to use his description of the Synagogue rituals from the same website.

The permission to reproduce copyrighted materials for use from "The Twelve: The Lives of the Apostles After Calvary" by C. Bernard Ruffin was extended by Our Sunday Visitor, 200 Noll Plaza, Huntington, IN 46750. 1-800-348-2440. Website: www.osv.com. No other use of this material is authorized.

Materials reproduced with permission from "Atlas of The Bible", copyright © 1981 by the Reader's Digest Association, Inc., Pleasantville, New York. www.readersdigest.com.

Excerpts from "Basic Judaism", copyright © 1947 by Milton Steinberg and renewed 1974 by David Joel Steinberg and Jonathan Steinberg. Reprinted by permission of Harcourt, Inc.

Permission from Perseus Books Group to reprint excerpts from "To Pray As A Jew" by Rabbi Hayim Halevy Donin. Copyright © 1980 by Rabbi Hayim Halevy Donin.

Permission from Leen and Kathleen Ritmeyer to use line art and "A Pilgrim's Journey" from their book "Secrets of Jerusalem's Temple Mount." Copyright © 1998 Biblical Archaeology Society.

Permission from Michael Olteanu to reproduce "The Lord's Prayer" in Aramaic and English from the www.christusrex.org website. Copyright © Christus Rex, Inc.

Permission to use numerous excerpts *(see Bibliography)* from various articles in Biblical Archaeology Review from Biblical Archaeology Society. www.bibarch.org.

Thanks

To Michael Olteanu @ www.christusrex.org/www1/pater/JPN-aramaic.html for his help with the Aramaic pronunciation of The Lord's Prayer.

To Leen and Kathleen Ritmeyer for their thoughtful permission to use material from their fine book "Secrets of Jerusalem's Temple Mount".

To Dr. John McRay, professor of the New Testament at Wheaton College Graduate School, for his kind permission to use illustrations from his outstanding book "Archaeology & The New Testament".

To Richard Nowitz for permission to use his photographs of the reconstruction of the Talmudic house from the archaeological dig at Qatzrin in the central Golan, Israel.

To Marina Banai of the Yigal Allon Centre's "Man in the Galilee" Museum, Israel, for her help in obtaining a photograph of the "Jesus Boat".

To all of the many authors and publishers of works quoted for permission to use this material in this book *(see separate listing on the previous pages)*.

To Dick Mauch, my old friend from Bassett, Nebraska, for inspiration and the use of his reference material lovingly collected over the years.

To Roger Sedlacek, a friend and former co-worker, for the loan of some of his reference material, notably a dog-eared copy of Henri Daniel-Rops from which I gained so much information and insight.

To Jim Clark and Bill Aurelius of Nashville, TN who gave me excellent and thoughtful suggestions on content.

To my eldest son, Michael, for the drawings he did for this book.

And, finally, thanks to Alice, my wife of 46 years, for her patience and proof-reading help as I made this joyful journey of discovery about my Lord and Savior.

<u>Dedication</u>

Dedicated to my brother and sister Christians and Jews, who share alike the rich traditions of ancient Judaism, and to our Muslim friends with whom we share the sacred history of the Temple Mount.

And with a special remembrance to 12-year-old Agnes Gonxha Bojaxhiu, an Albanian of Skopje, Serbia who committed herself to God at that age and who we would later know and love as the saintly Mother Teresa of Calcutta. She was born not far in distance or in time from my maternal grandparents' birthplace in Uljanik, Croatia, then a part of Hungary. She was kind to me and touched my life.

Table of Contents

Introduction

I am an ordinary person just like most of you, who has been drawn to learn more about what it must have been like to live and work in Galilee and the surrounding area during the time of Yeshua bar Yosef *(Aramaic)*, Joshua ben Joseph *(Hebrew)*, who we now call Jesus The Christ *(Greek)*. I must leave it to theologians and more learned people than me to interpret the religious life that Jesus lived, preached about and started. Countless thousands of people over two thousand years have now had their own opportunity to do so. And billions of us since those days have helped keep him hanging on his agonizingly bloody cross as he pays for our sins. For he still hangs there on that rough tree, you know, somewhere in time, the sharp points of the crown of thorns digging cruelly into his bloodied, sweating head, the excruciatingly painful nails into his feet and wrists. His body twisting and turning in agony as he tries to draw a breath into his tortured body. Are you present at the crucifixion?

I have a simple faith in this God/Man, this itinerant Galilean preacher born into this ordinary life that he chose. My prayer almost daily is that when I die I may be permitted to return to share a meal with him, his mother, his foster father, and his immediate family at their small home in Nazareth. That would be my idea of Heaven. Perhaps I could be a stranger just coming upon his small village nestled in the rolling hills in my dusty travels, and the boy who would become a Saviour would still be in his teens. Perhaps knowing what I have in store for me is what has led to the research and writing of this small book.

I have not made any of this up, but have harvested it from the works of many others who are listed in the text and the appendix for those of you who would like to look into these fascinating times in more detail. This is not a novel, it is simply a collection of facts about those days. Days, that when compared to geologic time, happened only a heartbeat back. I leave it to you to fashion your own dream. If even for one split-second Jesus, Mary or Joseph becomes a live flesh and blood person to you as you read this book, then my work will have been successful. Such an epiphany happened to me many times as I researched and wrote this small book, and it is an unexpected flash of insight, warmth and a tremendous blessing from God. I have been so richly blessed to be allowed to write this book.

What an interesting concept. That the Creator of all of this synchronicity in the vast beautiful Universe and beyond would become a very ordinary person like you and me so that he would know what it was like to live on this Earth. To be tempted, to get blisters, to loose his temper, to question himself, to have a headache, to be hated, to love, to be loved, to weep, to be hungry, to be frustrated, and to work outside the accepted behavior of his time. To learn what it means to have "free will." Jesus was a seeker. I have been one, too. By virtue of the fact that you've picked up this book I know you are a seeker as well.

I hope you have found where you are most comfortable with the Lord. If you currently have no church, I invite you to read these pages, learn more about Jesus, talk to him in your heart as a friend and ask his guidance, and then start visiting various denominations until you find people and a place that make you want to get up each weekend and worship. You know, Jesus and his first followers were all Jews, but they, too, found the place where they were most comfortable with our heavenly Father, and there they spent the remainder of their lives. My own Father found the Lord on his deathbed. And I was there holding his hand. It is never too late for you to begin seeking Him.

So this small book is to honor this young teenage Galilean boy, Yeshua bar Yosef, who wears his carpenter's rule behind his ear in the tradition of the day. Perhaps with a curl or two of planed wood in his hair and sawdust on his sun-burned nose as I approach his small stone house in the late afternoon, and as I hear his Mother call to him to wash up. I hear him laugh at something his foster father says out in their workshop as I approach. But that will have to wait until I take my last breath. Until then, I trust that you will enjoy this short journey back in time.

Yours in Christ,

Dick Lattimer
Cedar Key, Florida

Preface

Once in a small country in the mideast, a teenage girl over 90 miles from home, who said she was still a virgin, gave birth to a baby boy in a stable cave in a small southern village in that land. It was probably 6 or 7 B.C., according to how you try to correct the error that was later made in the calendar.

The boy grew up in another small village in the hilly northern part of this small country and worked as a craftsman with his foster father who had married the young girl in spite of the shame of her being pregnant. All three during their lives professed to having Angels, or even God, talk to them either in dreams, or while they were wide awake.

Some people would later say that this little boy fulfilled more than 300 prophecies about his birth and life foretold over the 1,500 years it took to write what we Christians now call the Old Testament.

When the boy was in his late 20's, beyond the age when he should have been married, according to the custom of the times, he decided to become a wandering preacher. And he convinced a group of common people like himself, most of whom were ordinary fishermen and some who were relatives, to go along with him on his journeys throughout the countryside. And so they wandered the land for about three years, talking to people and healing their ills. Some people even claimed that he performed miracles.

The young self-proclaimed preacher and healer eventually went off the "deep end" according to the religious and political leaders of his day. And so to stop his verbal attacks on their Temple ways and their age old beliefs they sentenced him to death. They beat him, forced a crude crown made out of thorns down on his head, humiliated him in front of his people, and even made him carry his own execution device to the small hill where they "took care of people like him". There they drove nails through his wrists and feet and let him hang on that dead tree until he was, too.

Some three days later, after he had publicly been pronounced dead and been buried in a borrowed hole cut in the limestone not far away, he was seen by some of his followers and in the 40 days that followed by more than 500 people who claimed that he had "risen from the dead". Hundreds of thousands laughed at this and called it a lie and a fakery. And so, the whole thing quieted down for a time. But then one of the people who had been persecuting his sorry bunch of followers, these religious fanatics of their day, suddenly decided that maybe they were right about this young man. And so this former tent-maker, a fellow by the name of Saul from a city called Tarsus, who learned to make the leather and black goat-hair shelters from his father, gave new life to the cause in the old principal of opposites. And so it went as time and the world meandered on. We would later know this fellow as a man named Paul, who met the Lord on the road to Damascus.

Today almost 2 Billion people on this wobbling blue planet say that they "believe" that this young man was actually who he said he was, the Creator of the Universe who decided to see what it was like to be born, live and die as a human being. His is the single largest religion in the world today, with 34% of the world's people saying they believe in him.

About 3 Billion other people believe in other prophets or faiths, and almost 800 Million people say they do not believe in any religion, while 150 Million say they are atheists.

So the followers of this young Jewish martyr from the small country on the eastern end of the Mediterranean Sea still have their work cut out for them if they are to continue to convince the rest of the world that this young baby boy born in a cave is who he said he was.

Perhaps this small book can nudge just one of you almost 4 Billion souls, who do not yet believe in this young man, or one of you 2 Billion "believers" who still have some doubts, gently into his corner to help him carry his sorry cross.

Will it be you?

1

His Name

When I recently asked a Roman Catholic priest friend what Jesus' real name was he reacted somewhat startled, as if everyone knew the answer to that. "You shall call his name Jesus" he paraphrased from the Gospel according to St. Matthew. At my suggestion that that was not really the original form of this man's name, he bristled.

Perhaps you feel the same way at the very idea. We are so very used to calling this God/Man, Jesus Christ, meaning Jesus the Messiah. But Christ was not this first century man's last name, it was derived from the Greek word *Christos*, which means the Anointed One. And as mentioned earlier, Jesus is the Greek form of his Aramaic name, Yeshua.

To quote another distinguished Roman Catholic priest, John P. Meier, professor of the New Testament at the Catholic University of America in Washington, D.C. and one of the foremost biblical scholars of his generation, writing in his 1991 book "A MARGINAL JEW, Rethinking the Historical Jesus", Father Meier tells us:

"Our English form of Jesus' name is derived from the Hebrew name Yesu, the shortened form of the earlier and "more correct" form Yesua, found in the late books of the Hebrew Bible. The name Yesua is in turn a shortened from of the name of the great biblical hero Joshua son of Nun, in Hebrew Yehosua, the successor of Moses and leader of the people Israel into the promised land. "Joshua" was the ordinary form of the name used before the Babylonian exile. Among Jews after the Babylonian exile, however, "Jesus" *(Yesua and then later the shorter Yesu)* became the common form of the name, although "Joshua" did not die out entirely. "Jesus" remained a popular name among Jews until the beginning of the 2nd century A.D., when perhaps Christian veneration of Jesus Christ led Jews to stop using Yesua and Yesu as a personal name. They instead revived "Joshua" as the common form of the name, the form borne by a good number of notable rabbis. Thus, "Jesus" became a rare name among Jews after the 2nd century."

Father Meier goes on: "So current was the name Jesus that some descriptive phrase like "of Nazareth" or "the Christ *(Messiah)*" had to be added to distinguish him from the many other bearers of that name. The 1st century historian, Josephus *(Ed. Note: born just a couple of years after Jesus died)* , mentions some twenty or so men called "Joshua" or "Jesus" in his writings *(Greek uses the same form, Iesous, for both "Joshua" and "Jesus")*, not less than ten belonging to the time of Jesus of Nazareth...neither the name nor the fate of the Nazarene was all that unique...so important was it to use "Christ" *(Messiah)* as a distinguishing name for Jesus that, by the time of Paul in the mid-fifties of the 1st century A.D., "Christ" was well on its way to becoming Jesus' second name."

"The name Joshua /Yehosua originally meant "Yahweh helps" or "May Yahweh help." As often happened in the Bible, the original or scientific etymology was forgotten and a popular etymology was invented. In the case of Yehosua, the name was interpreted to mean "Yahweh saves" or "May Yahweh save." It is this popular explanation of the name that is reflected in the angel's remark to the dreaming Joseph in Matt 1:21: "You shall call his name Jesus, for he shall save his people from their sins.""

Henri Daniel-Rops, writing in "Daily Life in the Time of Jesus" wrote that "The Jews had no surname-it did not exist. This does not mean that the sense of family was not very highly developed among them: it was. A son necessarily bore his father's name, as among the Arabs of today. A man was called "son of so-and-so," ben in Hebrew and bar in Aramaic."

John W. Miller, Doctor of Theology, and Professor Emeritus of Religious Studies at Conrad Grebel College, University of Waterloo, Ontario simply states it this way in his fascinating book "Jesus at Thirty, A Psychological and Historical Portrait"— Name: Yeshua *(Aramaic),* Joshua *(Hebrew),* Jesus *(Greek).*

And so, Jesus' real name in his native Aramaic tongue in Nazareth in Galilee would have been Yeshua bar Yosef...in Jerusalem in Hebrew he would have been Joshua ben Joseph. Chaim Potok tells us that "in the Galilean Hebrew dialect of that day his name was probably pronounced Jeshua."

Sources for this chapter, and recommended reading for you:

Rev. John P. Meier, *A MARGINAL JEW, Rethinking the Historical Jesus.* © 1991 John P. Meier. The Anchor Bible Reference Library, published by Doubleday, New York, New York.

Henri Daniel-Rops, *Daily Life in the Time of Jesus, An authentic reconstruction of Biblical Palestine and the day-to-day lives and customs of its people.* © 1962 Hawthorn Books, Inc. 70 Fifth Avenue, New York, NY 10011. Mentor-Omega Book Edition, Published by The New American Library. Originally published in France by Librairie Hachette, © 1961.

Dr. John W. Miller, *Jesus at Thirty, a Psychological and Historical Portrait.* © 1997 Augsburg Fortress, Box 1209, Minneapolis, MN 55440.

Professor John Dominic Crossan, *THE HISTORICAL JESUS, The Life of a Mediterranean Jewish Peasant.* © 1991 John Dominic Crossan, Inc. Published by HarperCollins Publishers, 10 East 53rd Street, New York, NY 10022.

Giuseppe Ricciotti, University of Rome, *The Life of Christ.* Translated by Alba I. Zizzamia, Trinity College, Washington, D.C. © 1947 The Bruce Publishing Company, Milwaukee, Wisconsin. Imprimatur Michael J. Curley, D.D., Archbishop of Baltimore and Washington.

Chaim Potok, *Wanderings, Chaim Potok's History of the Jews.* © 1978 by Chaim Potok. A Borzoi Book published by Alfred A. Knopf, Inc. Distributed by Random House, Inc. New York, NY.

David Stern, Translation by, *Jewish New Testament, a translation of the New Testament that expresses its Jewishness.* © by David Stern. Published by Jewish New Testament Publications, Inc., P.O. Box 615, Clarksville, MD 21029.

E.P. Sanders, *The Historical Figure of Jesus.* © 1993 E.P. Sanders. Published in the U.S. by Penguin Books, Inc., 375 Hudson Street, New York, NY 10014.

2

His Language

Imagine yourself standing with the late afternoon sun at your back as you look out over the Sea of Galilee at the distant hills on the eastern shore. The wind has died down and gentle waves lap at Simon bar Jonah's 26 foot long fishing boat anchored just a few feet offshore. On this day Simon stands in the water holding the sturdy fishing craft steady for the man standing above him on the back steering platform of the boat. *(Luke 5:1-3)*

The man's long hair is blowing in the breeze and he is smiling as he looks over the 20 or 30 people standing with you on the shore. You have heard that he is back in town from one of his travels and you have come to hear what he has to say this young evening. This is not the first time you have come down here to the anchorage in Capernaum to hear him, nor will it be the last. Something about the man intrigues and appeals to you. He does not shout on these quiet evenings, nor wave his arms as so many do. But he talks quietly, so that people listening almost have to strain to hear what he has to say, but in so doing they remember his words and the message he is trying to give them. The man now says something quietly to Simon bar Jonah that you cannot quite hear and receives a smile and a laugh in return.

And then he again looks out at the assembled group and directly into your eyes with the smile still on his face. He then begins to speak as if his words are intended only for you. Your eyes are locked on his, and you cannot look away as you smile back at him.

What would any of us living today give to be able to step back into time and be that person that Jesus is speaking to that late afternoon along the shore as Peter stands in the water holding his boat? What would his precious voice sound like? And what would his words sound like when he uttered them? Perhaps this is your moment that you have to look forward to someday.

Jesus and His Apostles spoke Palestinian Aramaic, a dialect of the Hebrew language of that day in their everyday conversation. It was an old language used throughout the mideast as the common language among countries, much like Latin was at a later time throughout Europe. Aramaic was the language of not only the Hebrews, but also the Syrians, Chaldeans and the Assyrians. By the 8th Century B.C. it was the major language from Egypt to Asia Minor to Pakistan. The Persian *(now Iranian)* government also spoke Aramaic in some of their Western provinces.

"The term Aramaic", according to the modern-day Assyrian website, "is derived from Aram, the fifth son of Shem, the firstborn of Noah. See Gen. 10:22. The descendants of Aram dwelt in the fertile valley, Padan-aram also known as Beth Nahreen. The language of the people of Palestine shifted from Hebrew to Aramaic sometime between 721-500 B.C.. Therefore, we know that Jesus, his disciples and contemporaries spoke and wrote in Aramaic. The message of Christianity spread throughout Palestine, Syria and Mesopotamia in this Semitic tongue."

But Jesus and his fishermen friends would also have had to know Greek and perhaps even Latin in addition to Hebrew. Now let's turn to someone with more authority than I to look into this a bit more.

Writing in the Biblical Archeology Review in 1992 "Did Jesus Speak Greek?", Joseph A. Fitzmyer, a Jesuit Priest and Professor Emeritus of Biblical Studies at Catholic University of America in Washington, D.C. states: "That Jesus spoke Aramaic there is no doubt. By Jesus' time numerous local dialects of Aramaic had emerged. Jesus, like other Palestinian Jews, would have spoken a local form of Middle Aramaic, called Palestinian Aramaic...Though Aramaic was the dominant language, it was not the only language spoken in Palestine at that time. The Dead Sea Scrolls reveal that a trilingualism existed in Palestine in the first and second century of the Christian era. In addition to Aramaic, some Jews also spoke Hebrew or Greek—or both...Greek, of course, was in widespread use in the Roman empire at this time. Even the Romans spoke Greek, as inscriptions in Rome and elsewhere attest. It is hardly surprising, therefore, that Greek was also in common use among the Jews of Palestine...Did Jesus himself speak Greek? The answer is almost certainly yes. The more difficult question, however, is whether he taught in Greek...That Aramaic was the language Jesus normally used for both conversation and teaching seems clear. Most New Testament scholars would agree with this."

"All four Gospels depict Jesus conversing with Pontius Pilate, the Roman prefect of Judea, at the time of his trial *(Mark 15:2-5; Matthew 27:11-14; Luke 23:3; John 18:33-38).* Even if we allow for obvious literary embellishment of these accounts, there can be little doubt that Jesus and Pilate did engage in some kind of conversation...In what language did Jesus and Pilate converse? There is no mention of an interpreter. Since there is little likelihood that Pilate, a Roman, would have been able to speak either Aramaic or Hebrew, the obvious answer is that Jesus spoke Greek at his trial with Pilate."

"Moreover, these specific instances in which Jesus apparently spoke Greek are consistent with his Galilean background. In Matthew 4:15, this area is referred to as "Galilee of the gentiles *(non-Jews)*." Growing up and living in this area, Jesus would have had to speak some Greek. Nazareth was a mere hour's walk to Sepphoris and in the vicinity of other cities of the Decapolis...Coming from such an area, Jesus would no doubt have shared this double linguistic heritage. Reared in an area where many inhabitants were Greek-speaking gentiles, Jesus, the "carpenter" *(tekton, Mark 6:3)*, like Joseph, his foster-father *(Matthew 13:55)*, would have had to deal with them in Greek. Jesus was not an illiterate peasant and did not come from the lowest stratum of Palestinian society; he was a skilled craftsman. He is said to have had a house in Capernaum *(Mark 2:15)*. He would naturally have conducted business in Greek with gentiles in Nazareth and neighboring Sepphoris...His followers, especially the fishermen Simon *(Peter)*, Andrew, James and John, would also have had to conduct their fishmongering in Greek with gentile customers. So Jesus almost certainly spoke some Greek."

"Another point sometimes made by those who contend that Jesus taught in Greek is that a number of Jesus' disciples had Greek names: Andrew, Philip and even Simon *(a Grecized form of Hebrew Sim 'on)*. Levi/Matthew, a toll-collector, would have had to deal with people in Greek *(Luke 5:27)*."

Today Aramaic is still spoken in small communities in Syria, Iran, Turkey and Iraq.

Thanks to the internet, all can now see what Aramaic writing looks like, as well as get some instruction in how to speak it. The following is reproduced with the permission of this website: www.christusrex.org/www1/pater/JPN-aramaic.html. Scholars believe that Jesus not only taught the Lord's Prayer during the Sermon on the Mount, but probably at other times as well. Perhaps you will hear him do it on that day when you stand looking into his eyes there on the shore at Capernaum.

The Lord's Prayer

In Aramaic

Abwoon d'bwashmaya,
Nethqadash shmakh,
Teytey malkuthakh.
Nehwey tzevyanach aykanna d'bwashmaya aph b'arha.
Hawvlan lachma d'sunqanan yaomana.
Washboqlan khaubayn (wakhtahayn)
aykana daph khnan shbwoqan l'khayyabayn.
Wela tahlan l'nesyuna.
Ela patzan min bisha.
Metol dilakhie malkutha wahayla wateshbukhta l'ahlam almin.
Amen.

In English with Aramaic Pronunciation Guide

Our Father in Heaven
A-voon de-vesh ma-ya
Hallowed be Thy Name
Nith-ka-dash smakh
Thy Kingdom Come
Tai-thai mal-koo-thakh
Thy Will Be Done As In Heaven So On Earth
Neh-way sev-ya-nakh Ai-ken-na de-vesh ma-ya
Give Us Bread For Our Needs
Up ber-ah hav-lan
from Day to Day
Lakh-ma de-soon-ka-nan
Forgive Us Our Offenses, as We
Yo-ma-na wush-vok-lan
Have Forgiven Our Offenders
khoe-baine ai-ken-na de-up
Do Not Let Us Enter into
khnan sh-vak-n el-kha-ya-ven
Temptation
Ula ta-e-lun el-nis-yoe-na
Deliver Us from Evil
Il-la pes-on min-boe-sha

For Thine is the Kingdom
Mit-thil de-de-lakh-ee
And the Power
Mal-koo-tha oo-khay-la
And the Glory
Oo-tish-boakh-ta
For Ever and Ever. Amen
El-a-lum all-meen. A-men.

Sources for this chapter, and recommended reading for you:

Rev. Joseph A. Fitzmyer, *Did Jesus Speak Greek?*   Biblical Archaeology Review, September/October 1992, Vol. 18, No. 5, pages 58-63.

The Assryian Website-http://www.aina.org/aol/

www.christusrex.org/www1/pater/JPN-aramaic.html.

3

His Writing

Again quoting Fitzmeyer-"The only thing that we are told that Jesus himself wrote, he wrote on the ground *(John 8:6-8)*—and the evangelist took no pains to record it."

Jesus did this when the Scribes and Pharisees brought the adulteress to him. Beginning with John 8:3 we learn: "And the Scribes and the Pharisees brought unto him a women taken in adultery; and when they had set her in the midst, they say unto him, Master, this woman was taken in adultery, in the very act. Now Moses in the law commanded us, that such should be stoned; but what sayest thou? This they said, tempting him, that they might have to accuse him. But Jesus stooped down and with *his* finger wrote on the ground, *as though he heard them not.* So when they continued asking him, he lifted up himself, and said unto them, He that is without sin among you, let him first cast a stone at her. And again he stooped down, and wrote on the ground. And they which heard *it,* being convicted by *their own* conscience, went out one by one, beginning at the eldest, *even* unto the last: and Jesus was left alone, and the woman standing in the midst. When Jesus had lifted up himself, and saw none but the woman, he said unto her, Woman, where are those thine accusers? Hath no man condemned thee? She said, No man, Lord. And Jesus said unto her, Neither do I condemn thee: go, and sin no more. Then spake Jesus again unto them, saying, I am the light of the world: he that followeth me shall not walk in darkness, but shall have the light of life." *(According to the Holy Bible, Masonic Edition, © 1940 by A.J. Holman Co., Philadelphia, PA)*

When Jesus lived people wrote on papyrus rolls. These were usually about 33-feet long. Papyrus grows 3 to 12 feet high and is a water plant and member of the sedge family. In the time of Jesus some of it grew along the Jordan River. In those days people soaked thin slices of its pith, then laid them crossways, put pressure on them then dried and scraped them, resulting in a surface that could be written upon. The pith of the papyrus plant is the soft, spongy tissue on the inside of the stems of the plant. The ancient Egyptians living next door to the Land of the Jewish People perfected this technique three thousand years before the time of Jesus using the plant that grew so abundantly along the Nile River in their country.

When papyrus was scarce, or too expensive, people would often write on the dried and scraped skins of goats or sheep. They used split reeds dipped in lamp-black and gum for pens. This was kept dry and moistened only when it was about to be used. They did not ordinarily use ink as we do today, although red ink was known in those days.

And so the only mention in the New Testament of Jesus actually writing was of his writing on the ground, but he certainly could have written down information on scraps of papyrus or skins about the dimensions of what people wanted built in the carpenter shop, and probably other things about his life or that of being a craftsman and son. However, just as the most common things today do not survive time, and that is what keeps antique shops in business, Jesus' most ordinary writings did not survive time. Or, if they ever were kept and did exist, they were destroyed or hidden by the anti-Christians or Christian martyrs over the last two thousand years. Perhaps some are yet to be found by a wandering goatherd, still buried and waiting for us in a cave in the Holy Land, just as was Babatha's skillet.

Sources for this chapter, and recommended reading for you

Rev. Joseph A. Fitzmyer, *Did Jesus Speak Greek?* Biblical Archaeology Review, September/October 1992, Vol. 18, No. 5, pages 58-63.

The Holy Bible, Masonic Edition, © 1940 by A.J. Holman Co., Philadelphia, PA)

4

His Galilee

When Jesus lived, Galilee was relatively small, measuring about 30 miles north to south, and 25 miles east to west. About the same size as a normal-sized county here in the eastern United States today. Josephus tells us that within this small area there were 204 cities and villages. Galilee is in the northern part of Israel.

One of those small villages up in the hills of Galilee was called Nazareth. Nazareth was only 100 yards by 400 yards large, perhaps 6 acres, contained about 35 stone houses, and no more than 300 people, according to several recent estimates from archaeological digs going on. It was in Nazareth that Jesus grew up and became a man. He would have lived there after returning from exile in Egypt from about the age of 3 until he left his Mother's home and moved to Capernaum to Peter's house at about the age of 30. Nazareth lies halfway between the Mediterranean Sea to the west and the Sea of Galilee to the east. A line drawn due east from Nazareth would hit the southern end of the Sea of Galilee.

Nazareth lies roughly on the same latitude up from the equator as Macon, Georgia; Dallas, Texas; Alamagordo, New Mexico; and San Diego, California.

And to keep things in perspective, the entire country that the Israelites lived in was just a bit smaller than the land size of New Jersey, about 145 miles in length from north to south, and only 25 miles wide at the north, about 87 miles wide at the south near the Dead Sea. Rabbi Stephen M. Wylen, in his book "The Jews in the Time of Jesus" tells us that "Before the Israelites entered the land, it was called the land of Canaan. After the Israelites conquered the land and absorbed its Canaanite inhabitants into their own group the land was known as the land of Israel. In Second Temple times *(when Jesus lived)* the name of the Jewish state was Judah." He also tells us that "The land of Israel lies on the southeastern shore of the Mediterranean Sea. The land of Israel connects Africa to Asia and Europe. As the bridge between three continents the land of Israel is strategically important..."

Map used with permission of Dr. John McRay© Baker Book House Company

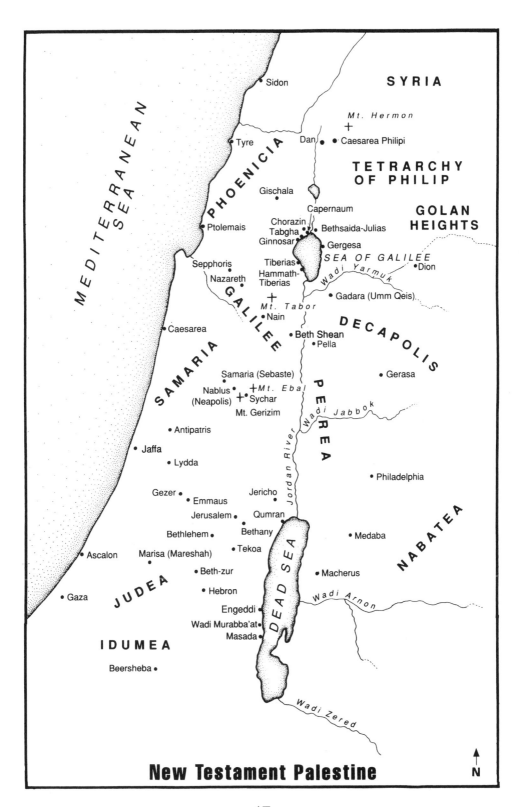

New Testament Palestine

17

Israel lies at the top of the boot-shaped Arabian Peninsula. On its west side lies the Mediterranean Sea, to the east lie Jordan and Syria, to the north Lebanon and to the south the Sinai Peninsula of Egypt. The Great Rift Valley, a giant break in the Earth's crust, runs from southeastern Africa up to Syria and cuts through Israel. The Jordan River runs down the Great Rift Valley, connecting the Sea of Galilee to the Dead Sea, southeast of Jerusalem. The Dead Sea is the lowest point on Earth at 1,286 feet below sea level. It is a salt water lake.

The population of Israel *(Palestine)* when Jesus lived was anywhere from 500,000 to 600,000. About the same number of people as live today in Vermont. And, according to www.christianityonline.com, about 18,000 of these were "clergy, priests and Levites."

Unfortunately for Jesus, or Joshua, as he was then called in Hebrew, his foster Father probably died sometime in his late teenage years and as the eldest son of the family it was up to him to take charge of the household and to be the bread-winner. There were evidently four younger brothers *(James, Joseph, Judas, and Simon)* and several sisters *(names never mentioned)*, along with their Mother, Mary, living in the house.

Some who would guard the idea of the perpetual viginity of Mary would argue that these other children were Joseph's by an earlier marriage, or that they were cousins, or related in some other way. By revealing this to you I in no way want to demean your vision of Mary, who has also been very special to me my entire life. My own Mother was named after Mary. I find this whole question both puzzling, mysterious and emotional.

Whatever your personal, or church-related beliefs about Mary, know that the teenage boy Joshua *(Jesus)* had his hands full helping to raise the family and keeping them in groceries. We can only assume that he did these things well for perhaps ten years or more, but then upon reaching 29 or 30 he decided that enough was enough and he left his Mother's house to go off on his own to begin his life's work. Anyone who has read even portions of the New Testament will know that relations were by then strained between Mary and her eldest son. Remember when she and her other "sons" went down the 20 miles northeast from Nazareth to Capernaum on the Sea of Galilee to bring the wayward Jesus home? When told that they wanted to see him, Jesus said: **"Who are my mother and my brothers? Here are my mother and my brothers! Whoever does the will of God is my brother, and sister, and mother"** *(Mark 3:33-35)*. It occurs to me that when God came to Earth in the form of a man he would have wanted to expe-rience all of the emotions of a normal earthling. The strained relations between Mary and her son at the time would not have been unusual in the human experi-ence, nor any other of the usual family dynamics that we all deal with in our every day lives. Why else would God come to Earth to see what it was really like to live as a "Man or Woman"? He wanted to feel what we, his creatures, feel.

But let's turn our attention back to Nazareth. Although it is true that to some it was a small "hick" town, it lay just 4 miles, a short walk away from what was then the Roman Capital of Galilee, Mary's traditional hometown of Sepphoris *(Zippori in Hebrew)* where, according to legend, she had lived with her mother and father, Joachim and Anna, before moving to Nazareth and marrying Joseph. It was the tradition of the day that girls married according to the Law as soon as they were physically able to do so, often at 12-and-a-half. The Virgin Mary was probably 14-years-old when she had Jesus. A boy usually married at the age of 18, although some waited until the age of 24.

Richard Batey, in the Biblical Archeology Review, included the description of the view of Sepphoris from Nazareth that Jesus would have seen as set down by Leroy Waterman of the University of Michigan who excavated at Sepphoris in 1931:

"Across the rolling uplands to the north the peak of snowy Hermon hangs like a fleecy cloud above the horizon; to the west, the blue Mediterranean shimmers under the afternoon sun like a vast molten mirror, while halfway between, in full view and only an hour's walk from Nazareth, lies the site of the city that at the beginning of the first Christian century reared its brilliant acropolis, Sepphoris, 'the ornament of all Galilee,' its capital and its largest and most ornate city, and at that time second only to Jerusalem in importance in all Palestine."

This bustling metropolitan area of Sepphoris within easy eyesight of Nazareth had 30,000 inhabitants-Jews, Arabs, Greeks and Romans. It had been partially destroyed by Quintilius Varus, the Roman Legate of Syria, to keep the city from falling into the hands of rebels against Rome led by Judas of Gamala after the death of Herod the Great *(Herod Antipas' father)* in 4 B.C.,when Jesus was probably 2 or 3 years old. But the city's history went back at least 100 years before that. And following it's destruction, it was immediately rebuilt by Herod Antipas during Jesus' youth and young manhood, while he and his carpenter father lived and labored just a short 4 miles away.

Sepphoris rises 250 feet up on a hill from the floor of the Bet Metofa Valley 700 feet below and northwest of Nazareth. Perhaps this was the source of Jesus' words **"A city set on a hill cannot be hid"** *(Matthew 5:14)*. The Biblical Archeology Review reported that "Sepphoris means 'bird' because it is perched on a hill like a bird." In addition to being the Capital of Galilee, second in importance only to Jerusalem, Sepphoris was also the Capital of Perea, a large territory to the east of the Jordan River, southeast of Galilee. Richard Batey, who helped James F. Strange, the veteran archaeologist from the University of South Florida, excavate Sepphoris in the 1980's, tells us in his book, "Jesus & the Forgotten City," that "Sepphoris became the nerve center for the government's control of Galilee and Perea. Political policy, military strategy, economic regulation and cultural affairs were administered from this seat of power. Influences from Sepphoris affected the people living in Nazareth as well as other satellite villages. Josephus tells us that Sepphoris was the largest and most beautiful city in the region."

Batey goes on to say that "the city plan, laid out on the Roman grid pattern adjusted to the contours of the land, has all the elements typical of a splendid Roman provincial capital—a main east-west street *(the Cardo)* leading to the Forum, Antipas' royal residence with its imposing tower that offers a breathtaking panorama, a 4,000 seat theatre, bath, archives, gymnasium, basilica, waterworks and other buildings." "The stage of the theatre itself was 156 feet wide and 27 feet from front to back."

Batey quotes a visit to Sepphoris with Strange as he describes a visit to the city. "The wall surrounding the acropolis ran in this direction. The colonnaded main street, bordered by shops and public buildings, ran west to intersect the major north-south thoroughfare." The city also had "markets, pools, fountains, public baths, ritual baths, a residential district and the royal palace of Antipas...at one time Sepphoris occupied 500 acres of land."

Dr. Strange's University of South Florida website also tells us that ancient Sepphoris had "ten synagogues...a Council Chamber, an Archive, two market places, temples, a city wall, a mint *(Sepphoris minted its own coins)*, an extensive aqueduct system, and a cemetery. It was also known for its old fort and for its spice shops."

Major trade routes converged in this valley, linking Sepphoris with the Greek cities of Antioch, Damascus, Petra and Decapolis. Also with the ports on the Mediterranean 18 or 20 miles to the west, such as Tyre and Sidon, and with Jerusalem, some 80 miles to the south. Jesus literally lived at the crossroads of the world of His day.

To think that with all of this construction going on during his lifetime within easy sight of Nazareth and within easy walking distance that Jesus and his foster father Joseph did not help build Sepphoris really takes a stretch of the imagination. They certainly must have played a part. How could they ignore the steady wages and years of uninterrupted work that was available just a short walk away? As Shirley Jackson Case, professor of the New Testament at the University of Chicago stated, "Very likely 'carpenter' as applied to Jesus meant not simply a worker in wood but one who labored at the building trade in general, and it requires no very daring flight of the imagination to picture the youthful Jesus seeking and finding employment in the neighboring city of Sepphoris. But whether or not he actually labored there, his presence in the city on various occasions can scarcely be doubted; and the fact of such contacts during the formative years of his young manhood may account for attitudes and opinions that show themselves conspicuously during his public ministry."

Remember, Jesus' grandmother and grandfather, Mary's parents, Joachim and Anna, probably lived in Sepphoris while he was growing up. It doesn't seem to be much of a stretch to think that even if Joseph chose not to work there, or, after Joseph died, that Jesus could still have labored there while he was a teenager and may even have lived with his grandparents on occasion without the need for the two hour walk each day back and forth to Nazareth. Perhaps returning home each Friday to celebrate the Sabbath with his Mother and family, bringing his weekly pay with him for their support. Even if Joachim and Anna had fled when Sepphoris was attacked and destroyed there is no reason to believe they would not have quickly returned "home" just as soon as it was safe to do so. Jesus' ties could have been deep, indeed, to metropolitan Sepphoris.

As a matter of fact, Batey goes on to remind us that "one of Jesus' followers was Joanna, the wife of Antipas' finance minister, Chuza. She followed Jesus about Galilee in the company of several other women, who together underwrote the expenses of his itinerant ministry (Luke 8:3). Joanna was certainly one person who could have told Jesus about the splendor in which Antipas and his court officials lived. The excesses and extravagances of the royal family stood in sharp contrast to the conditions of the poor peasants dwelling on the land."

Whatever Jesus' relation to Sepphoris was, you can be sure he visited it often, maybe even attending the theatre there, or even helping to build it. Batey reports that the floor of the stage was probably constructed of wood, and has not survived, but that "this raises the interesting possibility that Jesus and his father, being carpenters, may even have helped build the stage."

Sources for this chapter, and recommended reading for you:

Dr. Richard A. Batey, *Jesus & the Forgotten City, New Light on Sepphoris and the Urban World of Jesus.* © 1991 Baker Book House Company, Grand Rapids, Michigan 49516.

Dr. Richard A. Batey, *Sepphoris, An Urban Portrait of Jesus.* Biblical Archeology Review, May/June 1992 Pages 50-62.

Rabbi Stephen M. Wylen, *The Jews in the Time of Jesus.* © 1996 By Stephen M. Wylen. Paulist Press, 997 Macarthur Boulevard, Mahwah, NJ 07430.

Professor John Dominic Crossan, *THE HISTORICAL JESUS, The Life of a Mediterranean Jewish Peasant.* © 1991 John Dominic Crossan, Inc. Published by HarperCollins Publishers, 10 East 53rd Street, New York, NY 10022.

Andrew F. Beresky, Editor, *Fodors 91, Israel, With Excursions from Jerusalem and Tel Aviv.* © 1991 Fodor's Travel Publications, Inc., 201 East 50th Street, New York, NY10022.

The Associated Press, *Archaeological dig sheds light on Jesus' boyhood.* The Gainesville Sun, December 23, 1997, page 11A.

www.bibleinterp.com/articles/sepphoris.htm

www.christianityonline.com

www.israel-mfa.gov.il/facts/hist/arcsit3.html

5

His Home Sweet Home

As I write this there is a $60 million dollar plan underway to reconstruct a portion of Nazareth as it was in the days of Jesus. According to the Biblical Archeology Review, "Trimming olive trees, clearing underbrush and rebuilding terraces, 400 volunteers have begun work on a replica of Jesus' hometown. When construction is finished, a village of 35 one-room stone houses, inhabited by actors and storytellers in authentic garb, will illuminate the life and teachings of Jesus." All this is being done in an area in southwestern Nazareth and is being called Nazareth Village. As part of this work progressed the workers ironically "discovered the stone base of a wine press...subsequent excavations, revealing the remains of stone irrigation trenches, three stone watchtowers, a stone quarry and numerous agricultural terraces..there is a mounting body of evidence that these installations, these farms, were here in the time of Jesus...to give you some perspective, the area where Jesus grew up is about 500 meters, or a third of a mile, from the winepress."

What might the house that Joseph and Mary raised Jesus and the others in have looked like? Joseph and Mary would not have lived in a home this big when they were first married; however, as they prospered and grew older and had more children, it is reasonable to assume that they would have finally had a larger home, especially since Joseph and his foster son, Jesus, were carpenters and could have helped build them a larger one. Here is one description of a home from a similar village from just a century or two after the life of Christ. It comes from archeological work done by Ann Killebrew at the Talmudic-period village of Qatzrin (pronounced kats-reen) in the Golan. Like Nazareth, this village, too, was also the home of villagers and farmers. I have made just a few small artistic guesses from what Ann Killebrew has learned in my description of the house the Holy Family might have lived in. When you and I stop to think about it, our basic homes of today, without all the electronic and convenience items, are really no different from homes built 300 years ago in basic structure and use. So let us imagine that this was the home of Joseph the carpenter and his family. A carpenter of the time, it should be noted worked not only in wood, but also in stone, as part of the overall building trades of the day. One had to be versatile in order to make a living. Joseph's house was probably both his workshop and his family's dwelling. Imagine this as Jesus' teenage home.

Reconstruction of a Jewish home from the Talmudic Period not long after Jesus lived. The structure on the right is an outdoor oven used for cooking and baking. The entrance to the house is partially hidden to the left of the oven. This doorway let to the kitchen. The upper level was a sleeping loft.

Photo by Richard T. Nowitz
Used with permission

The house Joseph and his family live in for our visit today is built against the side of a hill, with the second story opening up at the back at ground level. Not all houses in the neighborhood had two stories, but since Joseph's workshop was there, he provided his family with additional room in an upstairs loft for sleeping in cooler weather on beds much like we have today. In the warmer months, they would often sleep on mats on the roof. One reached these flat roofs by way of stairways on the outside of the houses. Might the women also have hung the laundry up here to dry in what breeze could be found, above the dust of the roadway and yards? Photographs of similar flat-roofed houses in today's modern Israel show them doing exactly that.

These roofs had enough slope to them to carry off the rain, and low walls, or parapets, as commanded by Jewish Law. "For otherwise", as Daniel-Rops tells us, "If anyone should lose his footing and fall to the ground, thy house is polluted with blood, and the guilt is thine." These walls, by law, had to be two cubits *(3 feet)* high.

The house is made of limestone blocks and plastered with mud on the interior. In other areas it would have been built of local basalt blocks. But limestone was abundant here in Nazareth. It has openings in some of its outside walls to admit light, but no glass to keep out insects and the weather. Being a carpenter, Joseph and his sons would no doubt have built gratings or shutters to fit into the open windows.

We approach the house down a dirt roadway beaten down by the hooves of the donkeys and ox carts that pass this way, and by the sandals of the people who live here. A stone drainage ditch follows the road. According to the Talmud, public roads must be 24 feet wide, private roads just 6 feet wide. The front courtyard area of the house is partially covered with a low roof to protect it against the rain and sun. Here were the outdoor ovens that Mary and the girls of the family used to prepare the meals in during the warmer months in order to keep the heat out of the house. Here, too, were the grinding stones used in preparing the wheat or barley flour for bread. A fire would be built in the domed oven and allowed to burn down until the sides of the oven were very hot. The dough was a mixture of flour and water *(or olive oil)*. A piece of leaven *(fermented dough)* from a previous baking was kneaded into the new dough. After it rose, a small part of it was put aside for the next baking. The dough would then be applied against the sides of the oven, resulting in flat bread for the family. Out here they would also do the washing of clothes, dishes and cooking pots.

The main door into the house opens off this covered courtyard into a small kitchen area. The door "moved on hinges fastened with wooden pins...barred by wooden bolts, which could be withdrawn by check keys from the outside" according to Alfred Edersheim. On the right hand side of the door there is a small cylindrical case, the *mezuzah,* holding the commandments of God. Everyone touched this reminder of God upon coming or going and kissed their fingers where they had done so in a form of benediction, "The Lord shall preserve thy going out and thy coming in from this time forth, and even for evermore." The mezuzah held a parchment strip containing two sections of Deuteronomy 6:4-9 and 11: 13-21. These are two of the three sections of the Shema. The Shema and the Amidah *(also called the Tefillah-the prayer)* were the two most important prayers of Jesus' day. C.M. Pilkington in his book "Judaism" tells us that "Instead of the Hebrew letters rendered 'LORD' in English translations, a Jew will, out of reverence for the name and thus the nature of God, say *Adonai* which means 'Lord" or *Ha-Shem,* 'The Name'."

Deuteronomy 6:4-9:

"Hear, O Israel: the Lord our God is one Lord:
And thou shalt love the Lord thy God with all thine heart, and with all thy soul, and with all thy might.
And these words, which I command thee this day, shall be in thine heart:
And thou shalt teach them diligently unto thy children, and shalt talk of them when thou sittest in thine house, and when thou walkest by the way, and when thou liest down, and when thou risest up.
And thou shalt bind them for a sign upon thine hand, and they shall be as frontlets between thine eyes.
And thou shalt write them upon the posts of thy house, and on thy gates."

Then there is Deuteronomy 11: 13-21:

"And, it shall come to pass, if ye shall hearken diligently unto my commandments which I command you this day, to love the Lord your God, and to serve him with all your heart and with all your soul,
That I will give you the rain of your land in his due season, the first rain and the latter rain, that thou mayest gather in thy corn, and thy wine, and thine oil.
And I will send grass in thy fields for thy cattle, that thou mayest eat and be full.

Take heed to yourselves, that your heart be not deceived, and ye turn aside, and serve other gods, and worship them;

And then the Lord's wrath be kindled against you, and he shut up the heaven, that there be no rain, and that the land yield not her fruit; and lest ye perish quickly from off the good land which the Lord giveth you.

Therefore shall ye lay up these my words in your heart and in your soul, and bind them for a sign upon your hand, that they may be as frontlets between your eyes.

And ye shall teach them your children, speaking of them when thou sittest in thine house, and when thou walkest by the way, when thou liest down, and when thou risest up.

And thou shalt write them upon the door posts of thine house, and upon they gates:

That your days may be multiplied, and the days of your children, in the land which the Lord sware unto your fathers to give them, as the days of heaven upon the earth."

Here in this "kitchen" area the food was stored and the winter cooking and heating was done in another domed oven and chimney made of mudbrick sitting in a corner of the small room. The domed oven sat inside the chimney and had an opening at the top to create a draw and let the smoke rise, and an opening in the front through which cooking pots could be placed. Here Mary would prepare the meals and no doubt sit and sew, visit with her family and enjoy the warmth of the oven on cold winter or damp rainy days. Being a carpenter's house there would be no scarcity of benches and chairs to sit on. As in any normal house today, people no doubt liked to gather in the kitchen to watch preparations and to smell the delicious odors of the cooking food. And to talk to Mom. *(Isn't it nice to think of the Virgin Mary as "Mom"?)*

Here, too, were kept the cooking pots and dishes stacked inside one another, grinding tools, and a water jar or two. Mary would fill the water jug each day from the freshwater well located not far from the house, a gathering spot for the women of the small village, still known to this day as Mary's Well, the only freshwater well in Nazareth. This is also the time when the women shared the news of the day coming to them from along the nearby trade routes with the world, and the news of their own families. This was their support group. And in some churches today women still pattern their women's meeting groups after these gatherings at Mary's Well.

The kitchen area of the home. This indoor oven was used for cooking during bad weather, and to heat the house. Mud plaster would have covered the heavy stones on the floor to make a smooth surface.

Photo by Richard T. Nowitz
Used with permission

We now know from excavations of a hidden cave in the early 1960's, that women of that day also had iron frying pans. In 134 A.D. a woman by the name of Babatha, along with many of the people from her village En-Gid near the Dead Sea, hid from the approaching Roman army, led by Centurion Magonius Valens, as it searched for Jews and rebels in the area during the Second Jewish Revolt against Rome. The villagers hid in a meandering cave in the hills not far away. The Romans followed, camped above them and eventually starved them to death. It was not until the early 1960's when the area was discovered and searched that they found the legal documents and personal belongings of Babatha. Among her hidden things were her iron frying pan, an iron sickle, four wooden bowls, a metal mirror, a pair of women's leather sandals, keys, a chopper and knives. Babatha was a young widow with a son, Jesus son of Jesus *(no relation to Jesus the Christ)*. But it points out once again how very popular the name Jesus/Joshua was in those days. The bones of three men, eight women and six children were also found in this cave.

But back to our visit to the Holy Family's house in Nazareth. Here in Mary's small kitchen, next to the oven's drying warmth, would also be kept the storage jars full of "lentils, wheat, barley, millet, coriander, Egyptian beans, white beans, onions, and turnips." Cucumbers, cabbage, peas, and chickpeas were there in season as well. Here, too, might be sesame seeds and figs in their own containers. The salted, dried, or pickled fish would also be here, or kept back in the storage cave in the back of the house that the home had been built around. The cave's constant temperature would also be a good place to store vegetables and fruits during their season, as well as the wine.

The kitchen is lighted by small portable oil lamps, some sitting on wall shelves, others on floor stands. There were many kinds of oils to choose from to burn in them-olive oil, "sesame oil, nut oil, radish oil, fish oil, colocynth oil" and so on. The oven burned the remains of olives after pressing when they could be obtained, or dried animal dung.

Shelves hang from the ceiling for the storage of perishable things that Mary wants to keep from insects, rodents and household animals. And strings of garlic and other herbs hang from the ceiling, or shelving, as in a modern day kitchen.

In this small, cozy kitchen Mary cooks such things as the "young meat" of goats, lambs, and calves, although beef was rarely available to the common people at the time. And, of course, pork was never eaten, being forbidden by the religious law, as was camel and hare. Chicken from the chicken pen at the back of the house would also have been used in soups and stews or even roasted or fried in olive oil, as would antelope, deer, ducks, geese, pigeons, partridge or quail whenever they could be found at the market or obtained by hunting with bow and arrow, sling or snare. And any animal taken while hunting had to be bled well in order to satisfy the religious rules. A lamb that was roasted had to be done so over the wood from the grape vines. There were no turkeys or guinea hens in that country in those days, they were imported later.

Ordinary people did not have meat everyday, just as was common with my own Maternal Grandmother and Grandfather who came to this country from a small farming village, Uljanik, Croatia, in what was then a part of rural Hungary in the early 1900's. Meat was special on Sunday's to them, and for my widowed Grandmother to buy a chicken and make chicken paprika with rice and homemade noodle and farina dumpling soup was a special treat even in my own childhood. We are, after all, not so far removed from Biblical times in our own traditions and folkways.

Soups and stews in those days were probably made much like we do today with vegetables, onions, lentils and meat. Perhaps thickened with wheat or barley flour that Mary had ground. No recipes survive. But one can imagine a wintertime meal of thick vegetable soup and fresh-baked bread from the oven. Can you smell those wonderful odors there in Mary's kitchen, and hear the fire crackling in the oven? And, of course, there would have been the many meals of fish the family would have had from their fishermen friends at the nearby Sea of Galilee. The best-tasting was musht, the so-called St. Peter's fish. Musht is very good when fried. Fresh fish had to be eaten immediately, but salted or dried could be kept for awhile. The "fishes and loaves" fish of the hillside miracle were probably dried fish.

Eggs were always abundant from one's own chickens or from the merchants in the small town and were a very common food. That is debated by some historians, but makes sense to me, so I include it. Bread and cheese, or bread and fruit might also be eaten when little else was available. Bread was often dipped into honey, olive oil or into salt. I should point out that bread was never to be cut, but rather torn or broken. "It was to be treated with respect", according to Henri Daniel-Rops.

Salads made of lettuce were also eaten. One would presume they also included onions and cucumbers, onions being very popular in those days.

And it takes no stretch of the imagination to see them using vinegar and olive oil for dressing, with olives as a special garnish. Since forks did not exist, these would have been finger foods. Or, they might have used the wooden spoons that Joseph could have made in his workshop.

There would also have been homemade cider and fruit juices to drink, as well as goat's or ewe's milk. And, of course, wine, often prepared 2 or 3 parts water to 1 part wine. There were all kinds of wine available from the many vineyards surrounding the area, including red wine of Saron, black wine, spiced wine made with honey and pepper. Invalids were often given old wine, water and balsam. There was wine of myrrh, wine in which capers had been soaked, wine spiced with absinthe and a cooling drink called vinegar, made of either unripened grapes or of the lees. Also palm wine, barley wine from Egypt and others. But no record of any white wine.

Foreign food imports that were sometimes available were apples from Crete, cheese from Bithynia, gourds from Egypt and Greece, and beer from Media or Babylon.

Deserts included melons, pickled olives, fruit such as apricots, pomegranates, raisins, dried or fresh figs and dates. Figs were often dried and pressed into cakes. During what we call August, September and October there would be fresh grapes. And there were walnuts, almonds and pistachios. Locusts pickled, or fried in flour or honey were also the favorite of some. Just as John the Baptist lived in the desert on locusts and wild honey, the people of those days had many ways to prepare these delicacies. Daniel-Rops tells us that "sometimes they were cooked rapidly in salt-water, and then they had a shrimp-like taste and some a shrimp-like color; and sometimes their heads and legs were taken off and they were dried in the sun. Once dry, they were either put up with honey or vinegar, or else ground to powder. This locust-powder, which tasted rather bitter, was mixed with wheat-flour to make a much esteemed kind of biscuit, rather like those which Chinese cooks produce under the name of "shrimp-bread".

Condiments of Mary's kitchen would have included mustard and salt. Pepper was expensive, having to be imported from India. There might also have been thyme, majoram, sage, mint, wild rosemary, parsley, caraway, coriander, cumin, rue, saffron, coriander, and dill. Onions, garlic and shallots were very popular. Historians tell us they liked their food highly seasoned.

Most families ate just two meals a day. At midmorning they ate and they ate again in the cool of the evening. Can you see Jesus and Joseph leaving home in the morning on their donkeys with some flat bread, olives and cheese in a cloth for their "lunch" as they went to their work in Sepphoris just a short ride away? I can. I can see the sun rising over their right shoulders as they slowly rode down the hill from Nazareth, across the valley floor, then up the hill that Sepphoris was located upon. Perhaps talking of what all they would be doing that day, and in the evening sharing what all had gone on that day. What the foreman had said about the Roman overseer. The earthly Father nurturing and loving the son for the heavenly Father who watched over them each day, and also Mary and the girls left back home to their own work, whether in the kitchen, the outdoor ovens, or spinning the thread or weaving the cloth in the shade of the family room. This is also when Mary would have had the time to quietly give her girls their own religious and hygiene instructions, whether they were daughters, stepdaughters, or cousins, depending upon your belief. As they worked and talked, just as mothers and daughters do yet today. Ritual purity was a very important part of their religion and everyday life.

The floor of the kitchen and the family room living area next to it that they worked in were of limestone, perhaps covered with mud plaster to make a smooth surface for walking and for cleaning.

Speaking of the room off the kitchen, it was called "a *traqlin* " in rabbinic litera-ture. It was the room where the family ate and "hung out" and may have been two stories high with the sycamore beams of the dirt thatched ceiling showing. A side door led off it to the outside. One interior wall was called a "window wall" because of several openings in it and permitted light and ventilation into the upstairs sleep-ing loft, as well as the downstairs sleeping and storage area. The second floor sleeping loft for the children was accessible by ladder, but due to the slope of the land, it, too, had a small door to the outside courtyard at the back of the house. This led to where I surmise Joseph would have had his roof-covered outdoor workshop.

There, too, might have been the walled-in outhouse used by the family, ashes from the fireplaces used as lime to take care of the human wastes.
And, we might as well speak of that delicate subject some more. We do not know if the common people used wooden outhouse seats much like those still used many places in the world today. But we do know for a certainty that stone toilet seats have been found from the 7th to the 6th centuries B.C. in the City of David, the oldest part of Jerusalem. This research was done by Jane Cahill and David Tarler, directed by Yigal Shiloh of the Hebrew University of Jerusalem during 1978

In the reconstruction, the room off the kitchen was used as a storage room. However, had the author lived in the house this convenient room to the kitchen and outside door would have been used a bedroom for the husband and wife.

Photo by Richard T. Nowitz
Used with permission

This ladder leads from the traqlin (family room/eating area) up to the sleeping loft. The table would be on the left and boards suspended above it hold perishable foods keeping them safe from rodents and household animals. The door into the kitchen area is also on the left of the ladder.

Photo by Richard T. Nowitz
Used with permission

This is the sleeping loft showing a reconstructed bed of the period. It would have had rope webbing. To the right is a mat covering the opening that leads down to the traqlin. Since this house was built on a slope, as were many also in Nazareth, the doorway at the end of the room led outside. It would have had a sturdy door. A domed chicken coop can be seen through the doorway..

Photo by Richard T. Nowitz
Used with permission

35

to 1985. Cahill and Tarler found one of these seats in a small cubicle appended to the House of Ahiel. The seat "was fashioned from a large block of locally available limestone, set into the floor over a cesspit. The cesspit was lined with plaster." This recessed toilet seat has a large round opening going in a straight line from top to bottom. "In addition, it has a small, irregularly shaped opening extending from the top of the seat and exiting to one side. Although it is doubtful that they had separate men's and women's toilet seats, this small hole may have been designed for male urination." The researchers report that "although large stone toilet seats such as those from the City of David are unknown from other sites in Israel, thin slabs of stone with large, keyhole-shaped openings set above shallow pits and identified as toilets have been found in at least two sites in nearby Jordan. If you would like to know more about this delicate subject and the research done in the residue of these ancient cesspits *(palynology, involving pollen; and archaeoparasitology, involving parasites)*, you are invited to see the May/June 1991 issue of Biblical Archeology Review magazine. But now, let us return to a description of the house.

We really didn't spend much time in the traqlin, or family/dining room. It would have had a table in it at which the men of the family would have been served and eaten first, then the women and children. Just as it is still done in much of the world yet today, even in my Hungarian Grandmother's tradition. Killebrew's excavations also found another food storage area at one end of this room as well, closest to the kitchen. Benches were very common in these rooms in those days, so it probably was how the family also sat at this table to eat.

The common people of the day ate off imported plates from Cyprus, from the western coast of Asia Minor and from North Africa according to Killebrew. Also, "large, locally manufactured bowls called kraters were probably used as serving dishes. Small hand-made clay cups were probably used for drinking." Cups with handles, looking much like modern coffee cups, have been found in excavations in Jerusalem from the time of the Roman destruction in 70 A.D., just 30 years or so after Jesus was crucified. Nahman Avigad who directed the digs in the Jewish Quarter of the Old City from 1969 to 1983 said in the November/December 1983 issue of Biblical Archeology Review that they found so many of these cups in almost every home they excavated that they must have been "as common as coffee cups today." They also found "several handmade stone vessels with multiple compartments...perhaps used as a serving dish for olives and relishes, or....as an individual dinner tray." Does this remind you of our modern relish trays or compartmentalized paper plates?

For relaxing the family could have sat on other benches along the walls, or on mats on the floor. One can see the young Jesus laying on a mat in this room, with a small olive oil lamp on the floor next to him as he learned his religious texts with his father Joseph, who had these responsibilities to his son, according to the Talmud-"to circumcise him, redeem him, teach him Torah, teach him a trade, and find him a wife."

I am guessing that Mary and Joseph would have slept in the downstairs bedroom off the kitchen and family room. That would have been closest to the front door to the outside and to the oven/fireplace. That's the room I would have chosen for my wife and me to sleep in. The wooden frame bed Joseph built would have resembled those of today according to Killebrew, with rope webbing and wool blankets. Privacy for this bedroom, and the loft upstairs where the children slept, would have been provided with hanging mats over the doorways woven of date palm branches. The children might have had beds, or may just have slept on woven mats with their woolen blankets.

And, now, let's step outside the back of the house and look at Joseph's workshop. Much of this description comes from Batey, who has done so much archeological work in the area.

I see Joseph's workshop being inside a fenced in area where he kept the family donkeys, or asses, that he and Jesus rode to work when they were helping on a project in Sepphoris. The donkeys would have had their own covered shed from the elements and the beating sun. Daniel-Rops tells us that "the ass was an integral part of Palestinian life. It was to be seen everywhere. There was no family, however poor, that did not own one of these long-eared servants...this was not the ass of our countryside, still less the tiny, pathetic donkey of Morocco, but the Muscat ass, big and strong, able to go his five and twenty miles a day quite happily, an ass whose coat is sometimes of so pale a grey that it might almost be called white—a beautiful creature, upon which Christ could make a noble entry into Jerusalem. For draught and for carrying, the ass had no rival...the horse was a much less useful animal...the only horsemen that Jesus saw would have been Roman soldiers."

Nearby there would have been a covered shelter for the chickens, or other fowl, who would roam the yard much like chickens do today on many rural farms. Pecking at gravel and insects. They would need room to nest and to lay their eggs, so this was no doubt close to the size of a modern day chicken coop. If you, as I, ever entered a chicken coop as a youth to gather eggs you know what a special peaceful place they could be, with the hens gently clucking as they did their act of creation. Did young Jesus have this wonderful experience, too? I'll bet he did.

Joseph would also have had a covered shed to work in when it was cold, or raining, perhaps with a small oven for heating where he burned the donkey's dung. Batey suggests that his sturdy oak workbench could have been carried outside during the long dry season. "Inside the shed, stacked in neat piles, are rough planks of different local woods—oak, pine, cypress and sycamore fig. For special projects, such as furniture and kitchen utensils, there is walnut, cedar, and olive wood.

The hand tools...are scattered over the work bench and hang on the wall of the shed. Most of these tools would be familiar to present-day carpenters. To lay out the design there is a ruler, a square, straightedge, chalkline, plumbline, level and marker or scriber."

Batey also says there would be an axe to fell trees for timber from the nearby forest, a large saw, hatchet, mallet and chisel, plane, knife, adze, and bow drill, the latter having been introduced from Egypt. There would be awls and gimlets to drill smaller holes into which the iron or bronze nails could be driven. Wooden dowel pins would hold the joints together. There might also be a wood lathe, driven by a bow-type device the carpenter, or helper, would pull to rotate the piece of wood being worked on.

As a reminder, the countryside during this period was covered with forests, not like it is today, having been denuded in the meantime by Arab and Turk marauders and conquerors, and Frankish Crusaders. That is what is so fascinating and wonderful about the efforts of modern Israelis to plant new forests where none now exist. At the time of Jesus, Daniel-Rops tells us, there were cypress and junipers upwards of 65 feet high. "But the oaks and the terebinths were the really typical trees of the Palestinian forest and they were also very often standing alone or in clumps. As forests, they stretched from Carmel to the hills of Samaria and Galilee, and even as far as Bashan. They belonged to several species, the vallonia oak of at least fifty to sixty-five feet in height, and the smaller evergreen kermes and gall oaks...still more usual were the bushy, branching terebinths or turpentine-trees, whose leaves, which gave off a penetrating scent, were not unlike those of a walnut tree. The carob was also very common...oriental planes, evergreen holm oaks, pistachio trees and wild olives." And there were the Egyptian sycamores, almond trees, the pomegranate and the date-palm. "As for the pasture land, it had the same mixture of meadow-grass, fescue, couch-grass and dandelions that one finds today." There were saffron crocuses, tulips, hyacinths, gladioli and narcissus, and of course, the lilies of the field...which were probably really the crimson gladiolus or the red anemone. Our white lily that we like to have in our homes at Eastertime to remind us of the Lord's passion was probably not a wild, but rather a cultivated garden flower, just as the rose was in those days.

"A carpenter in Nazareth," Batey writes, "manufacturers a variety of items for the local market. Basic household furniture includes tables, chairs and stools, beds, lamp stands and storage chests. Farm implements made for peasants and tenant farmers are plows, threshing boards, winnowing forks, yokes for oxen, and even carts and wagons." Carpenters would also have hewn out the ceiling beams, and built the doors, door frames and windows. Then, too, the farmer might ask the carpenter to help build him a barn for storing his harvest or his animals.

Daniel-Rops tells us that the early Christians even used a carpenter's adze (the ascia of the Romans) to form their secret symbol...the sign of the Cross.

How many of these tools Joseph and Jesus might have taken with them in a tool bag over the back of their donkey's each day when they went to work in Sepphoris or elsewhere in their area is anyone's guess, no doubt depending upon the job that they would be working on that day. But like the two beloved carpenters, Alan and Tony, that I have working in my own family today, they would certainly have brought their tools back home with them each evening to save them from the thieves working among them, or the robbers of the night around the construction sites in Sepphoris. Regrettably, little has changed in that regard in 2,000 years.

Some say that their work as carpenters, as with the other skilled craftsmen of their village, would be interrupted each year during harvest time when all would pitch in to help.

And, whether Jesus and Joseph were so busy working on projects in Sepphoris that they could only work on their neighbor's furniture and other needs in the evening is anyone's guess. But they could not, by law, do any work on the Sabbath.

That they were both carpenters, *naggars* in Aramaic, there is little doubt. It was the tradition of the father to teach the son his own trade and for the son "not to forsake the trade of the father". And it was Jesus who referred to the carpenter's trade in Matthew 7:4 when he said, **"How is it that thou canst see the speck of dust which is in thy brother's eye, and art not aware of the beam which is in thy own?"**

Also in this courtyard next to Joseph's workshop, or at the side of the house, there probably was a small kitchen-garden with a fig tree for shade. Mary and her flock could have raised lentils, beans, onions, shallot, leek, egg-plants, red and green peppers, cucumbers, pumpkins, melons, lettuce, chicory, endive, cress, puslane and parsley. These were all mentioned as being popular kitchen-garden vegetables in those days by Daniel-Rops. There most certainly would have been a bench under the fig tree.

Perhaps Jesus helped weed his Mother's garden while she sat on that bench in the shade and sang or hummed to him. Do you suppose? Can you hear her gentle song?

Sources for this chapter, and recommended reading for you:

Dr. Ann Killebrew and Dr. Steven Fine, *Qatzrin, Reconstructing Village LIfe In Talmudic Times.* Biblical Archeology Review, May/June 1991, Vol. 17, No. 3. Pages 44-56.

Jane Cahill, Professor Karl Reinhard, David Tarler and Peter Warnock, *Scientists Examine Remains of Ancient Bathroom.* Biblical Archeology Review, May/June 1991, Vol. 17, No. 3. Pages 64-69.

Henri Daniel-Rops, _Daily Life in the Time of Jesus, An authentic reconstruction of Biblical Palestine and the day-to-day lives and customs of its people._ © 1962 Hawthorn Books, Inc. 70 Fifth Avenue, New York, NY 10011. Mentor-Omega Book Edition, Published by The New American Library. Originally published in France by Librairie Hachette, © 1961.

Professor Anthony J. Saldarini, _Babatha's Story, Personal archive offers a glimpse of ancient Jewish life._ Biblical Archaeology Review, March/April 1998, Vol. 24, No. 2. pages 28-37, 72-74/

Nahman Avigad, _A Craft Center for Stone, Pottery, and Glass, Jerusalem Flourishing._ Biblical Archeology Review, November/December 1983, Vol. IX, No. 6. Pages 48-59.

C.M. Pilkington, _Judaism._ © 1995 C.M. Pilkington. "Teach Yourself Books" NTC Publishing Group, 4255 West Touhy Avenue, Lincolnwood (Chicago), Illinois 60646. The "Teach Yourself" name and logo are registered trade marks of Hodder & Stoughton Ltd. in the UK.

Dr. Richard A. Batey, _Jesus & the Forgotten City, New Light on Sepphoris and the Urban World of Jesus._ © 1991 Baker Book House Company, Grand Rapids, Michigan 49516.

Dr. Richard A. Batey, _Sepphoris, An Urban Portrait of Jesus._ Biblical Archeology Review, May/June 1992 Pages 50-62.

6

His Sea of Galilee

The "Sea" of Galilee is actually a lake about 13 miles from north to south and 7 miles across. It has a surface area of just 64 square miles. It is a fresh water lake and is some 686 feet below sea level with a maximum depth of 157 feet. It is part of the Great Rift Valley that extends all the way south into Kenya in Africa. The Sea of Galilee is protected on the west and southwest by the hills of Galilee and in its mideastern side by the cliffs of the Golan Plateau, now known as the Golan Heights. As a result of being so protected the temperatures here in the wintertime average around 57 degrees Fahrenheit and in the hot summers about 88 degrees Fahrenheit. About 15 inches of rain falls in this area, almost all during about 50 days in the winter, in short, but violent showers. *(See Mark 4:35-41.)*

There were at least 15 busy man-made "seaports" located around the lake during the time of Jesus. The historian of that day, Josephus, tells us that there were 230 fishing boats working the Sea of Galilee in those days. Josephus was born in 37 A.D. and even worked for a time in Galilee, so we can probably rely on his estimates. His real name was Yosef bar Mattathyahu, before he adopted the Roman-sounding name of Flavius Josephus under which he wrote his histories. The Sea of Galilee was called Lake Gennesareth in ancient times, as well as Lake Tiberias, and Yam Kinneret in Hebrew.

Today the village of Bethsaida lies 1.5 miles north of the Sea of Galilee; however, in Jesus' time the water level was higher and Bethsaida was on the shore. It was the birthplace of Simon, Andrew, James, John and Philip. It was also where Jesus walked on the water, healed a blind man *(Mark 8:22-26)* and fed the multitude *(Luke 9:10-17)*.

When Jesus was about 30 years old he left his family in Nazareth and walked downhill to the northeast over to Capernaum on the western shore of the Sea of Galilee, saying, **"A prophet is not without honour, but in his own country, and among his own kin, and in his own house."** *(Mark 6: 4)* It was time for Jesus to "hit the road."

Capernaum was by then the home of the fishermen Simon bar Jonah *(who we now call St. Peter)* as well as his brother Andrew bar Jonah *(another of the 12 Apostles).* Levi bar Chalpai *(who we now call St. Matthew)* and his brother James bar Chalpai *(also of the original 12)* lived in Capernaum as well. Both were civil servants.

So Capernaum was the center of Jesus' ministry. He lived here in Peter's house and preached next door at the local synagogue. A 2,500-foot-long promenade ran along the length of the many piers and docks in the harbor just a few feet from Peter's house. Some of these black basalt rock piers are still visible today during the dry season and extended some 100 feet out into the lake. In some areas shallow pools have been discovered above the ground, about 10 feet by 11 feet where fishermen stored large live fish caught with dragnets. They would sell their fish to buyers directly out of these pools.

Matthew *(Levi)* was the toll collector here at Capernaum, and it is likely that he collected the "tax" from the fishermen when they pulled into the harbor in the morning after their night of fishing. In order to fish productively they had to fish at night when the fish could not see their nets, and when the lake was generally calmer.

At the time of Jesus there were about 1,000 people living in Capernaum according to John C. H. Laughlin writing in Biblical Archaeology Review, and it was the home to both gentiles and Jews. Laughlin tells us that "Capernaum is the Greek form of the Hebrew *Kfar Nahum,* which means the village of Nahum. The few architectural remains indicate that the buildings were spacious and well constructed of dressed stones and large amounts of plaster. This suggests that the village flourished economically during Jesus' time. Its location on the crossroads of important trade routes, the fertile lands surrounding it and the rich fishing available all contributed to its economic development."

There was also a Roman garrison there supervised by a Centurion. And one of the miracles performed in Capernaum by Jesus was when he healed the Roman Centurion's servant. According to the Gospel by St. Matthew *(8:5-13)* the Centurion said, *"Lord, I am not worthy that thou shouldest come under my roof; but speak the word only, and my servant shall be healed."* Of course, Jesus healed the servant, and this expression of faith on the Roman's part later became an important part of Christian worship. It is still in the Roman Catholic Mass today, *"Lord, I am not worthy that thou should come under my roof, say but the word and my soul shall be healed."*

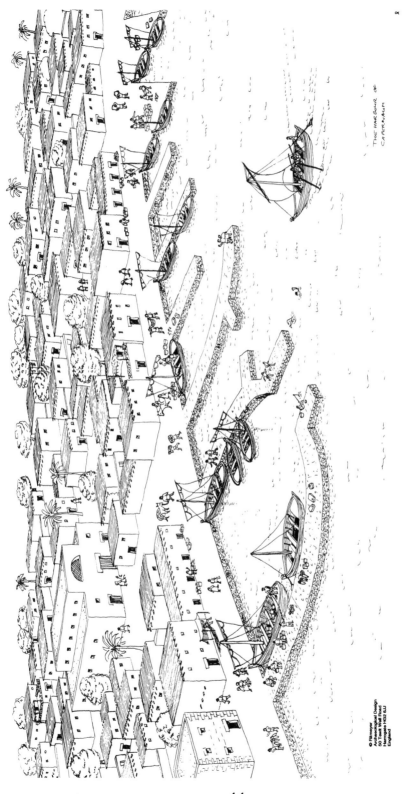

The harbor at Capernaum during the time of Jesus. Drawing by archaeologist Dr. Leen Ritmeyer. A 5,500 Foot-long promenade lined the shore. The remains of these unusually-shaped piers can still be seen during dry seasons. The synagogue where Jesus preached (John 6:59) is at the upper left (it has 3 doors and a raised central roof). St. Peter's house is between the synagogue and the harbor. According to Matthew (8:14-16) and Mark (2:1) this is where Jesus lived in Capernaum during his ministry.

Drawing by Leen Ritmeyer
Used with permission

Jesus often preached and taught at the synagogue in Capernaum. And it was here that he first uttered the words that would become the basis for the Sacrament of Christian Communion. **"Whoever eats my flesh and drinks my blood possesses eternal life, and I will raise him up on the last day. As the living Father sent me...he who eats shall live because of me. This is the bread which came down from heaven."** *(John 6:54-58)*. And, of course, Jesus repeated this instruction to his Apostles at the Last Supper.

One of the blessings of modern archaeology is finding ancient holy sites. And the Franciscans began work in the 1960's that has eventually led to the discovery of the original Synagogue that Jesus taught in. The fact that there were the remains of a Synagogue at the ruins of Tell Hum *(Capernaum)* have been known since 1838 from work done by the American Edward Robinson. In 1866 more excavations were done by the London-based Palestine Exploration Fund headed up by Captain Charles Wilson. He was the one who correctly identified the area as the site of Capernaum. But then after Wilson left the area builders and Bedouins started looting the site of its stones and so in 1894 the Franciscan Order bought the property to protect it. Father Gaudentius Orfali and his Franciscans started excavating the synagogue from 1921 to 1926. They resumed work in 1968 under the direction of two other Franciscan Fathers, Virgilio Corbo and Stanislao Loffreda. Work was also done by the Italians who discovered a 4th-century church built over St. Peter's House. Peter's house was only 84 feet from the synagogue, facing the entrance to the synagogue, which by tradition faced Jerusalem. Eventually this synagogue was dated to the 2nd-3rd Century.

But then in the further revealing of this great mystery story, the Franciscans discovered a lower wall of plain black basalt blocks, without mortar, under the beautiful shimmering white limestone walls of the 2nd-3rd Century synagogue. After many trenches were dug under the existing limestone synagogue, and under much fill and debris, the excavators discovered a "patch of rude cobbled pavement of black basalt". Lying on it were fragments of pottery dating to the 1st Century. And pottery under the cobbled pavement dated from the 3rd Century B.C. to the latter half of the 2nd Century B.C. More work was done and eventually the four foot thick black basalt walls of the original synagogue that Jesus taught in were found. The synagogue that our Lord worshiped in and instructed us in was 60.7 feet wide, 79.4 feet long and contained 4838 square feet. It was built of "hammer-dressed boulders of uniform size, without mortar." Based upon other 1st-Century synagogues it is assumed that benches lined three sides for the elders to sit on.

The others who attended the synagogue would have sat on mats on the floor, or also on benches. Other areas of the synagogue would have been used as a dining hall, a hostel, a school and for meetings.

"Although the synagogue was open three times a day for those who wanted to pray, special services were held on market days, Mondays and Thursdays. The Sabbath was the regular day for services, and most people attended on that morning." This we learn from Dr. John McRay and www.christianity.com a website source that goes on to tell us that on the Sabbath, "a minion *(group of 10 men over the age of 13)* was required to begin the services. Unlike temple services, these assemblies were characterized by simplicity. There was no official participation by priests or Levites, and no sacrifices were offered. Instead, services were conducted by ordinary members of the community."

The source for the information on this website is the Mishnah, the collection of rabbinic laws written not long after the death of Jesus. So we can probably assume that the synagogue services he participated in were not too much different then those described here. Close your eyes for a moment and see and feel his presence there, as he sat quietly there inside the synagogue with his fishermen friends from Capernaum alongside the shore of the Sea of Galilee. Can you see him? I can.

"The Sabbath service likely began with the congregation standing, facing toward Jerusalem, and reciting prayers beginning with the Shema *(Deut. 6:4)*...other prayers were then said, which became known as the Shemoneh Esreh...after the prayers came the essence of the synagogue service, the reading of the Torah. The hazzan *(attendant)* of the synagogue took the scroll from the ark and offered it to the first of seven selected readers. The selection was read carefully, not more than one verse recited from memory."

"The reading, like the prayers, was done while standing. Priests and Levites, if present, were given the honor of reading the Torah and pronouncing the priestly benediction, which had to be spoken in Hebrew. The Torah was read first, then the Haftorah, accompanied by a continuous translation into Aramaic...only one verse at a time could be read from the Law before translation, and three verses for the Prophets."

"Following the reading of the Law and Prophets, a sermon was given by someone invited by the hazzan. Preaching was not the prerogative of any one group or class of people. Jesus, for example, preached in the Nazareth synagogue."

"Whether the custom of seven readers was adhered to in Nazareth in Jesus' day is not known. If so, he must have been in the last group to read because he read from the Prophets rather than the Law, and then he immediately gave the sermon *(Luke 4:16)*. It does seem, however, that he selected his own passage to read *(4:17)*."

"The preacher closed the sermon with a brief prayer. On leaving the synagogue service it was customary for each person to give alms for the poor. Since presents as well as money were acceptable, the porch of the synagogue might be littered with various gifts."

One can just see Jesus leaving Peter's house, where he lived while he was in Capernaum, and walking over next door to teach in the Synagogue wearing his wool tallit *(prayer shawl)* over his head with blue horizontal stripes at each end and with tzitzit *(fringes)* at each of its four corners, blowing in the breeze. The fringes are to remind Him of God's Commandments *(Numbers 15:38-41)*. When putting on the tallit Jesus would probably have said the prayer that is still said today-"I am here wrapping myself around with a tallit to which tzitzit are attached, in order to carry out the command of my Creator...And just as I cover myself with the tallit in this world, so may my soul deserve to be clothed with a beautiful spiritual robe in the World to Come, in the Garden of Eden." A small tallit *(tallit katan)* is still worn by some traditional Jews as an undergarment throughout the day.

Luckily St. Peter's House also gave up it's mysteries to the excavators. When the Franciscans started excavating what they thought was an ancient church, they discovered that it had been built over the remains of another building that had also been an even earlier church. Grafitti on the walls reads "Lord Jesus Christ help they servant." and "Christ have mercy." All in all, over a hundred graffiti were scratched on the plaster walls most in Greek, but also some in Aramaic, Syriac, Latin and Hebrew. Also, various forms of crosses, a boat, and a monogram that may be using the letters of Jesus' name.

Eventually it was discovered that this early small church was really built in a domestic residence and that the original room had been 21 feet by 20 feet. The house had been built around 63 B.C. of "large, rounded wadi stones of the rough black basalt that abounds in the area." No mortar was used here either, as in the construction of the Synagogue Jesus taught in. The roof was probably "made from beams and branches of trees covered with a mixture of earth and straw." The floor was also paved in the black basalt stones with large spaces in between.

These are the remains traditionally identified by archaeologists as St Peter's house in Capernaum.

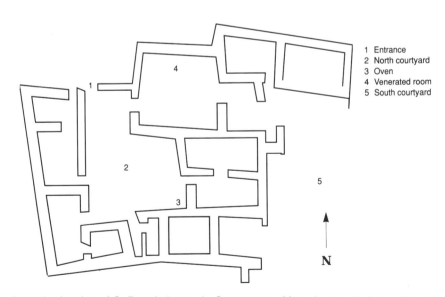

1 Entrance
2 North courtyard
3 Oven
4 Venerated room
5 South courtyard

N

A schematic drawing of St Peter's house in Capernaum. Many homes in those days were built around a courtyard with rooms off the house opening into the courtyard. The venerated room is believed to be where Jesus lived while staying with St. Peter (Simon bar Jonah).

48

The house had two interior courtyards. One on the north side of the central house "was probably the main area for the family that lived here. A round oven, where the family's food was no doubt prepared, was found in the southwest corner of this courtyard. This courtyard was surrounded by smaller rooms on the north and west. On the south was the largest room of the house." This was the main living area and later became the main room in the first church built on the site. A door off this room's south wall led into the other courtyard that "may have been used for animals or for work areas. Curiously enough, several fishhooks were found beneath one of the upper pavements from the later house-church." This was the only excavated house in Capernaum with plastered walls and floor. This was done to add illumination to a room.

"This house church," according to James F. Strange and Hershel Shanks writing in Biblical Archaeology Review, "survived into the mid-fifth century. Then, precisely over the now plastered central room, an octagonal church as built. Sometime between 381 A.D. and 395 A.D. a Spanish nun named Egiria visited the site and reported in her diary that she had seen the house of St. Peter which had been turned into a church: *"In Capernaum a house-church (domus ecclesia) was made out of the home of the prince of the apostles, whose walls still stand today as they were."* A similar report appears in the diary of the anonymous sixth-century A.D. Italian traveler known as the Pilgrim of Piacenza."

And, so, we now know the house Jesus lived in and the Synagogue He taught in during His days in Capernaum. What other exciting things do we yet have to discover and learn in the future? Isn't it thrilling to contemplate what future archaeologists yet have to painstakingly uncover for us about Jesus and His life?

A bit of interesting trivia for those who are fascinated by seashells, is that archaeologists have also found piles of Murex shells buried in Capernaum. The people living in Jesus' time punctured these seashells with bone needles and extracted the royal purple dye that they contained. They were a valuable commodity of the day.

A mile or two south of Capernaum there is an area of warm mineral springs along the lake known as Tabgha, shorthand for Heptapegon, meaning "Seven Springs" in Greek. These warm waters in the wintertime attracted a fish species called musht, also called "St. Peter's Fish". In the winter the fishermen from Capernaum worked in this area where the fish congregated. It was here at a prominent rock at the warm springs that Jesus formally met his Apostles for both the first and the last times. The rock is known as the "rock of the primacy of Peter".

According to tradition, it was also at Tabgha that Jesus multiplied the two fishes and five loaves of bread. "And he commanded the multitude to sit down on the grass, and took the five loaves, and the two fishes, and looking up to heaven, he blessed, and brake, and gave the loaves to his disciples, and the disciples to the multitude.. And they did all eat and were filled: and they took up of the fragments that remained twelve baskets full. And they that had eaten were about five thousand men, beside women and children." *(Matthew 14: 19-21)*

Another couple of miles down the lake is Magdala. In Hebrew it was known as "Fish Tower" and in Greek as Tarichea, "The Place Where Fish Are Salted". It was also the home of Mary Magdalene, the woman that Jesus befriended and who was present when he was crucified. She was also the first person Jesus appeared to after his Resurrection *(John 20: 11)* The historian Josephus claims that there were 40,000 people living in Magdala during the time of Jesus. While this may be overstated, the town was an important one in Galilee, and probably the most important one on the lake *(Sea of Galilee)* at the time. Its most dominant industries were weaving and fishing.

In the winter of 1986, just a mile north of Magdala, and perhaps 6 miles south of Capernaum where Jesus lived for a time, a two-thousand-year-old fishing boat was found not unlike the one Jesus would have sailed in with the Apostles on the Sea of Galilee. It does not take too big a stretch of the imagination to think that Jesus may even have seen or ridden in this ancient fishing boat. Two brothers, Moshe and Yuval Lufan from Kibbutz Ginosar discovered the boat's outline in the muddy lake bed during a particularly long drought. The boat was painstakingly excavated by the Israel Antiquities Authority under the direction of Shelley Wachsmann with the help of numerous volunteers. Due to the fragile condition of the boat, it had to be encased in fiberglass supports and covered with polyurethane in a technique pioneered by Orna Cohen. It was then floated to the nearby Yigal Allon Museum where it underwent almost ten years of a conservation process in order to protect its waterlogged timbers. For all of those years it "soaked in a pool of heated polyethyline glycol *(peg)*, a syntheic wax that replaced the water in the timber's cells." Tons of the peg were donated for this process by the Dow Chemical Company of Midland, Michigan. This process was completed in June 1995. To learn more about this process you can check the Museum's website at http://mahal.zrc.ac.il/ancient-boat/.

In 1986 during a severe drought this fishing boat was discovered in the Sea o Galilee not far from where Jesus lived in Capernaum with his fishermen friends. It was painstakingly preserved in a 14-year-long process and is now on display inside the Yigal Allon Centre's "Man in the Galilee" Museum in Isreal. The boat is 26-1/2 feet long, 7-1/2 feet wide, and 4-1/2 feet high.

Photo © courtesy of the Yigal Allon Centre
Israel

The boat was constructed of the ancient "mortise-and-tendon" joints held together with wooden pegs. The boat is 26-1/2 feet long, 7-1/2 feet wide and 4-1/2 feet high. It has a rounded stern. Both the bow and aft ends of the boat most likely originally had platforms. Most of the boat was constructed of cedar planking and oak frames, but there were five other kinds of woods also used-sidar, aleppo pine, hawthorn, willow and redbud. Evidence of a mast were found, but it could also have been rowed by four rowers, two on each side, with another fisherman in the rear working the steering rudder. A boat of this size could easily have contained Jesus and his Apostles. In those days the average size of Galilean men was just 5 feet, 5 inches tall and about 140 pounds. Josephus also tells us that boats like this could carry up to 15 people. Since Jesus was a carpenter by trade, it is likely that he could also have helped build or repair fishing boats of this kind. Perhaps he even did this while he lived next to the lakeshore in Capernaum between the travels he undertook during his ministry. For an idea of how large these boats were, get out a tape measure and lay out the outline of one of these boats. They were not little rowboats, but large working-size fishing vessels capable of standing up to all but the worst sudden storms on the Sea of Galilee. Can you smell and feel the wind and sea spray in your face as you journey across the Sea of Galilee with Jesus and his fishermen in their boat?

This particular boat was dated to the first centuries of the BCE/CE era *(Before Common Era-Common Era)*, including the time that Jesus lived using radiocarbon tests, a study of the hull construction techniques and pottery found along with the boat. The radiocarbon analysis dates the boat even more precisely between 120 BCE *(BC)* and 40 CE *(AD)*.

In February 2000, the "Jesus Boat" was moved to a permanent home inside the Yigal Allon Centre's "Man in the Galilee" Museum.

There were 18 species of fish in the lake, with 10 of them being commercially valuable. The catfish, having no scales, could not be eaten by the Jews. It was also called the mustached fish and sometimes grew to four feet long, weighing 25 pounds. The sardine was the smallest of the commercially caught fish, as it is still today where it makes up over half of the yearly catch from the lake. Sardines were preserved by pickling, and the main port for this process was at Magdala. They were an important part of the diet of the country. Then there are the three species of carp-like Barbels. The Long-Headed Barbel looks something like a trout and feeds on mollusks, snails and sardines. The Kishri variation also feeds on sardines. Both of these species are good to eat; however the third species, the Hafafi, eats decaying matter found in the mud and is not very good eating. The largest category of fish are the five species of musht, which means "comb" in Arabic, because their long dorsal fin looks like a comb. The largest of this species is the Tilapia, or white musht. It can reach a length of 18 inches and weigh about 4-1/2 pounds. It has relatively small bones and is easy to eat. As we said earlier, it is the fish known as St. Peter's fish. Musht are best when fried, Barbels best when boiled.

The Apostles who were fishermen had three kinds of nets at their disposal, the seine, the cast net, and the trammel net. The seine was a dragnet 750 to 1,000 feet long, about 25 feet high at its center and 5 feet high at its wings. The bottom was weighted with sinkers, the top had cork floats. It was taken out in a boat, about 100 yards or so from shore, then deployed parallel to the shore. Fishermen at both ends then slowly dragged it in towards shore trapping the fish in its netting.

The cast net could be held and thrown by one fisherman. We have scores of fishermen here in our tiny community of Cedar Key *(population 668)* who still use this type of net. Its diameter in Jesus' time was usually 20 feet or so. It, too, has weights on the bottom portion and quickly sinks, also trapping the fish. Various sizes of netting were used depending on whether one was seeking sardines, or larger fish. Simon *(later called Peter)* and his brother Andrew were using cast nets when Jesus told them to **"Follow me and I will make you fishers of men."** *(Matthew 4:19)*

The third kind of net was the trammel, and it is still used on the Sea of Galilee today. It consists of three "walls" of netting, with smaller netting on one panel. The fish would swim into it, become entangled and could not back out. This type of net was usually 500 feet long and also featured leaded weights at the bottom, cork or gourd floats at the top. The "walls" were usually 6 feet high. It, too, was strung parallel to the shore. The fishermen would then get between the shore and the net, splash the water with their oars, stomp on the boat with their feet, and frighten the fish into swimming toward deeper water, directly into the entrapping net. They might do this 10 to 15 times a night, and end up with 100 to 200 pounds of edible fish.

The fish the Apostles caught, often with Jesus with them, were either eaten fresh, or were salted, dried or pickled for later use.

Sources for this chapter, and recommended reading for you:

Mendel Nun, *Cast Your Net Upon the Waters, Fish and Fishermen in Jesus' Time.* Biblical Archeology Review, November/December 1993, Vol. 19, No. 6, Pages 46-56, 70.

Mendel Nun, *Ports of Galilee, Modern Drought Reveals Harbors from Jesus' Time.* Biblical Archeology Review, July/August 1999, Vol. 25, No. 4, Pages 18-31, 64.

Shelley Wachsmann, *The Galilee Boat, 2,000-Year-Old Hull Recovered Intact.* Biblical Archeology Review, September/ October 1988

Professor John C. H. Laughlin, *Capernaum, From Jesus' Time and After.* Biblical Archaeology Review, September/October 1993, Vol. 19, No. 5. Pages 54-61 & 90.

Professor James F. Strange and Hershel Shanks, *Synagogue Where Jesus Preached Found at Capernaum.* Biblical Archaeology Review, November/December 1983. Pages 200-207.

Professor James F. Strange and Hershel Shanks, *Has the House Where Jesus Stayed in Capernaum Been Found?.* Biblical Archaeology Review, November/December 1983. Pages 188-199.

Professor Steven Mason, *Will the Real Josephus Please Stand Up?* Biblical Archeology Review, September/October 1997. Pages 58-65, 67-68.

Gaalya Cornfeld, *Josephus, The Jewish War.* © 1982 by Massada Ltd., Publishers, Givatayim and Gaalya Cornfeld, Tel Aviv, Israel. published in the United States by Zondervan Publishing House, Grand Rapids, MI 49506.

http://mahal.zrc.ac.il/ancient-boat/

7

His Education

According to Wolfgang E. Pax, the director of the Institute for Bible Research on the Via Dolorosa in the Old City of Jerusalem, writing in his book "In the Footsteps of Jesus", "His father must have taught him the well-known *"Sh'ma"* *(Hear, O Israel)* as set down in Deuteronomy: "Hear, O Israel: The Lord our God is one Lord; and you shall love the Lord your God with all your heart, and with all your soul, and with all your might. And these words which I command you this day shall be upon your heart; and you shall teach them diligently to your children, and shall talk of them when you sit in your house, and when you walk by the way, and when you lie down, and when you rise. And you shall bind them as a sign upon your hand, and they shall be as frontlets between your eyes *(6:4-8)*.""

Rabbi Joshua ben Gamala, in the year 60 B.C. started the tradition of making sure that all Jewish children were educated by setting up the system of teachers for them in every area of the country.

Rabbi Stephen M. Wylen tells us that Simon bar Shetah, who was a leading Pharisee, and who might have been a brother of Queen Salome, established schools "for the universal public education for Jewish boys." Rabbi Wylen tells us that this began at the age of 5. "The children sat before the teacher all day. He read them a verse from the Bible, translated it and explained its meaning. The children repeated after the teacher, in this way learning the text, its translation, and how to live by it. At the age of ten, children completed their education in scripture and were apprenticed to their future jobs. A fortunate few, mostly the children of the wealthy, but also some dedicated scholarship students, went to a higher academy to study the laws and teachings of the sages. Some Christians of today prefer to think of Jesus as formally educated, even as having spent hidden years studying intensively with the sages of Israel. Other Christians prefer the image of Jesus without formal education, a simple man of the people whose words were directly inspired by the holy spirit."

Jesus would have referred to his father Joseph as "Abba", the Aramaic word for father. And, of course, he would later refer to God as Abba as well. His mother Mary he would have called "Imma" *(Eema)*, the Aramaic word for mother. The Jewish father would begin to teach his sons when they were three years old, and at five years of age start instructing them on the Hebrew Bible beginning with the Book of Leviticus or they would be sent to the school attached to the local synagogue, and the law decreed that there could not be more than 25 students in a class. If more, then an assistant teacher had to be hired. How our teachers of today wish they only had to have 25 students in a classroom.

Since the Holy Family did not return to Galilee from Egypt until Jesus was about 3, shortly after the age when children in those days stopped suckling at their mother's breasts, then Joseph must have begun instructing Jesus as soon as he was "back home" in Nazareth. I can see him now, carrying the young boy through the front door to the house in his arms, pausing as he showed him how to touch the *Mezuzah,* explaining what it contained, and how important it was to do it everytime he passed through the doorway. Jesus would have remembered these lessons, I am sure, since one of my own earliest memories is of my father carrying me in his arms into our house some 65 years ago when I, too, was about 3 years old.

Was Joseph perhaps also building this home at the same time, or did he return to one he had already begun constructing 3 years earlier for his betrothed when they had to flee Herod's fury after the baby was born in Bethlehem where he and the 14-year-old Mary had gone for the Roman Census so that taxes could be assessed? Historians tell us Jesus was born there in the year 6 or 7 B.C. Jesus was circumcised, according to Jewish law, when he was 8 days old. Also according to the law, a woman was considered unclean for forty days following the birth and was not allowed to leave the house or touch any holy objects. Then she had to travel to Jerusalem, only about five miles away, "to be pronounced clean by the high priest on duty at the Gate of Nicanor, which led to the temple; poor people had to sacrifice a pair of turtledoves...*(and)* the firstborn was consecrated to the service of God, which was described as being 'presented in the temple'", according to Wolfgang Pax. He also tells us that Mary and Joseph moved into a small stone house at that time instead of returning to Nazareth. But then they were warned by an Angel that Herod, who lived just 3 miles from the cave Jesus had been born in, was in a rage at this newly born "King of the Jews" that he had heard about and was going to slaughter all the male children under the age of two to be sure he killed him.

Joseph then took Mary and Jesus into Egypt. "According to an ancient tradition it is said to have been Heliopolis, north of Cairo," Wolfgag Pax tells us. One can imagine and feel the fear they felt as they rode their donkeys away from the land they knew and loved, no doubt with water bags and provisions over the asses backs as they left in the dark of early morning so no one could tell which way they had gone. Mary with a newborn, perhaps not yet physically recovered from the birthing. How uncomfortable and full of fear she must have been, this 14-year-old woman-child. How painful for her physically and mentally, riding off into the unknown in the darkness.

When Herod died painfully, probably of cancer, in 4 B.C., it was safe to return. But in doing so Joseph stuck close to the shore of the Mediterranean until he safely got far enough north with his family to turn to the east and Nazareth. By doing so he skirted the populated areas of Judea, also passing through Samaria before cutting northeast toward home. He feared being apprehended by Archelaus, Herod's son, who had taken over as ruler of Judea.

In such a small village as Nazareth, the synagogue would not have been a long walk from the house for Jesus. Presumably he had other children his own age in the neighborhood that he would walk to school with, perhaps Mary would go along at first on her way to the Well to get water, just to make sure, you know, that he did not get lost. Like a modern mother, perhaps not quite ready for her little boy to already be old enough to be off to school.

The teacher was usually the minister, or *chazan,* of the synagogue. They were always married men, and they were paid by the congregation, not by the individual students, so they did not show favoritism to the rich. Teaching occurred before 10 a.m. in the morning, then was discontinued due to the heat until 3 p.m. And according to Alfred Edersheim "For similar reasons, only four hours were allowed for instruction between the seventeenth of Thamuz and the ninth of Ab *(about July and August)*, and teachers were forbidden to chastise their pupils during these months." Parents also could not send their children to schools in neighboring villages, they had to attend the school in their own village. And they were also encouraged to teach their children how to swim.

When being taught, the students either stood in a semi-circle around the teacher, or sat the same way around him on the floor, or ground if outside, so that all could see the teacher.

After learning his alphabet at the age of 6, Jesus and his classmates would spend the next 7 years learning the Scriptures by rote. They would "proceed from the book of Leviticus to the rest of the Pentateuch, thence to the Prophets, and lastly to the Hagiographa" according to Edersheim. Memorizing was a very important part of their education.

You will note that there are age differences mentioned by our various sources for this chapter. Whatever the age, it is important to know that this is probably what occurred in the life of Jesus.

At the age of 13 the boys would come of age and have their *Bar Mitzvah.* They would then be allowed to attend the Synagogue with the men of the village. Men always sat separately from the women and children in the synagogue. Ruffin tells us that these students were "taught little, if any, mathematics, history, science or geography." But Daniel-Rops tells us that "Language, grammar, history and geography, or at least the rudiments of them, were all studied in the Bible. 'It is in the Bible,' says Josephus, 'that the finest knowledge is to be found, and the source of happiness.'"

Incidentally, this term *Bar Mitzvah* applies only to Jewish boys when they become 13 years of age and is translated to mean "Son of the commandment". You will recognize the word "Bar" *(son of)* from the Aramaic version of Jesus' name-Yeshua bar Yosef. Jewish girls are thought to mature earlier than boys, and they receive their *Bat Mitzvah (daughter of the commandment)* today when they are 12 years of age. This recognition of girls coming of age is a rather recent tradition in the Jewish religion according to several sources.

Some rabbis would not teach girls, but since Mary knew her Torah well, we can assume that she might have had some influence in the village to insure that girls were also taught, even if in a separate class. The carpenter of the village was an important person in the lives of those who lived there, so it isn't too unreasonable that Mary may have had some influence with the rabbi as far as education for the girls of the village is concerned. Daniel-Rops tells us that "Every man is required to teach his daughter the Torah." Further, that "If we may judge by the example of the little Virgin Mary, it may be supposed that many Jewish girls knew the Holy Scriptures as perfectly as their brothers; for when she spontaneously spoke the splendid words that we know as the Magnificat, so many biblical echoes came to her that one can distinguish no fewer than thirty of them (*Luke 1:46-55).*"

The 14-year-old Virgin Mary spoke the Magnificat when she visited her kinswoman Elizabeth, who lived in a village near Jerusalem, who was with child with the baby John, shortly after the Angel had told Mary she, too, would bear a son. When she arrived and Elizabeth heard her voice, her baby leapt in joy within her womb and she said to Mary, "Blessed art thou among women, and blessed is the fruit of thy womb!" This is a portion of what Roman Catholics today call the "Hail Mary". And Mary's reply to Elizabeth has since been called the Magnificat *(Luke 1:46-55)* :

"My soul doth magnify the Lord,
and my spirit hath exulted
in God my Savior;
because he hath regarded the lowliness of
his handmaid;

For lo, from henceforth, all generations
shall call me blessed;
because he who is mighty hath done great
things to me;
and holy is his name.

And his mercy is from generation unto generations,
to them that fear him.
He hath shown might in his arm;
he hath scattered the proud in the conceit
of their heart.

He hath put down the mighty from their thrones,
and hath exalted the lowly;
he hath filled the hungry with good things;
and the rich he hath sent empty away.

He hath succored Israel his servant,
being mindful of his mercy,
as he spoke to our fathers,
to Abraham and his seed forever."

As loyal Jews, Joseph and Mary would have gone with their family, along with the others from their village who could travel in a group for safety from highway robbers, down to Jerusalem each year for the Passover Festival. This was a two or three day walk, and by today's highway is about 88 miles. We all remember the

59

story from Luke when Jesus made this trip with his family when he was 12 years old and disappeared. They found him discussing religion in the Temple with the teachers there. When they admonished him, he said: **"Did you not know that I must be in my Father's house?"** *(Luke 2:49)*

After the age of 15 young boys could enter the Academies, and go further with their religious instruction. But that meant going to study in Jerusalem according to Daniel-Rops, and we have no mention that this is what Jesus did. Nor do we have any record of what he did between the age of 12 and 29 or 30 when he began his itinerant ministry.

Let's not leave the children of this age before we touch on what they did for fun. Girls played with dolls, and archaeologists have found evidence that the children of that day also played hopscotch. They had balls and rattles to play with, and small birds and animals made out of pottery, with some on wheels. They also had whistles, hoops and spinning tops. Older kids played a form of checkers. Since it was not unusual for people of that day to have hardwood bows and arrows at home for hunting, it would not be a stretch of the imagination to say that the children of Jesus' time, just as the children of today, may have been fascinated with archery and may also have had small bows and arrows to play with, no doubt with blunt, rounded tips so they could not injure one another.

Children in those days also played a game similar to jacks. And, I'll just bet that they had a few games they played that did not require any special equipment, like "hide and seek", or tag, or running races. And you don't think the little girls also played "house", too, do you?

Sources for this chapter, and recommended reading for you:

Dr. Alfred Edersheim, *Sketches of Jewish Social Life, in the days of Christ.* Wm. B. Eerdmans Publishing Company, Grand Rapids, Michigan.

Dr. Alfred Edersheim, *The Life And Times of Jesus The Messiah.* Wm. B. Eerdmans Publishing Company, Grand Rapids, Michigan.

Dr. C. Bernard Ruffin, *THE TWELVE, The lives of the Apostles After Calvary,* © 1984 Our Sunday Visitor, Inc., 200 Noll Plaza, Huntington, Indiana 46750.

Rabbi Stephen M. Wylen, *The Jews in the Time of Jesus.* © 1996 By Stephen M. Wylen. Paulist Press, 997 Macarthur Boulevard, Mahwah, NJ 07430.

Dr. Wolfgang E. Pax, *In The Footsteps of Jesus.* © 1970, 1975 by Nateev Printing & Publishing Enterprises, Ltd. P.O. Box 6048, Tel-Aviv, Israel

Henri Daniel-Rops, *Daily Life in the Time of Jesus, An authentic reconstruction of Biblical Palestine and the day-to-day lives and customs of its people.* © 1962 Hawthorn Books, Inc. 70 Fifth Avenue, New York, NY 10011. Mentor-Omega Book Edition, Published by The New American Library. Originally published in France by Librairie Hachette, © 1961.

8

His Clothing

Now let's speak of the clothes that Jesus and his family wore. Common sense tells us that they would have had everyday work clothes, and also special clothes that they wore to the synagogue, and for other special occasions such as weddings and funerals. Just as you and I do.

Their clothes would most likely have been made of wool or linen. Most of the wool in those days came from Judea, just to the south of Nazareth. Of course, wool comes from sheep, but it also can be made of goat's hair. The area around Nazareth was more known for linen made of the abundant flax grown there. Flax is a slender plant with delicate blue flowers and narrow leaves. The seeds are used to make linseed oil and fibers of the stems are spun into linen thread. The thread can then be woven into cloth. And, of course, the hair of the sheep and goat can also be spun into thread and the thread then woven into wool on the loom. Mary undoubtedly did both for her family, as well as sewing the clothes with needle and thread.

While he worked as a carpenter Jesus would have worn an undergarment known as a *saq,* in other words, linen underwear, perhaps like men's boxer shorts of today. Over that he would have worn a white, below-the-knee-length tunic with a girdle, or belt, around his waist. When working, walking fast or running he would have tucked the tunic up under his belt, "hitched up" his tunic, we might say. In those days they called it "girding up the loins". The belts were made of leather, cloth or even rope. Some had small compartments in them.

Women's everyday clothes were much the same, but probably embroidered and more colorful. They used vegetable or animal dyes. Yellow came from the saffron crocus, pink from promegranate bark, red from insects that lived on dwarf oak trees, and purple from the murex shellfish. Blue and brown were also popular colors. Women also wore linen undergarments, and wool tunics. Silk was used, but rarely, since it had to be brought in by caravan from far away. The Law forbid both wool and linen being used in the same garment. Women's tunics would probably have been longer then the men's and fuller. And rather than carry a purse, they often used cloth wrapped around their waist several times and kept their "women's things" in there. Perhaps a comb, some jewelry, some make-up, perhaps a snack. The Biblical expression "in the bosom" refers to this practice. They did wear bracelets and even earrings, but according to the Law could not pierce their ears. Rings were worn not only on fingers, but sometimes even in their noses and on toes and ankles. They sometimes wore chains around their necks, and they used hair-pins and had elegant combs. They also had mirrors.

Over the tunic, their basic garment, they wore a draped cloth that they called a cloak...a *talith.* Some were no more than two blankets sewn together, others had holes for the head and arms to fit through. This could be used as a garment during the daytime, as a blanket at night or even a saddle-cloth when they were traveling. They could also be used as collateral for loans, but according to the Law had to be returned to the borrower every night. Most Jewish looms were only three feet wide, so in order to make a cloak, two pieces of material had to be sewn together. Archaeologists have also dug up many examples of broaches that the Jews wore to hold their cloaks together, as well as what look somewhat like modern safety pins. Women's, of course, could have colored stones, or jewels, in them, making them part of their jewelry.

The women also wore ribbons in their hair, and shawls.

Edersheim tells us that "some ladies used cosmetics, painting their cheeks and blackening their eyebrows with a mixture of antimony, zinc and oil". And Nahman Avigad's archeological excavations in the Jewish Quarter of the Old City of Jerusalem uncovered the remains of a "glass factory" of Jesus' time. In it he and his staff found an abundance of what are called "kohl sticks". These are thin twisted glass rods that women used to apply the black paint, called kohl, to their eyes. They were twisted and look much like long modern screws; however, they have one end rounded, the other end pointed and were about six inches long. Among Babatha's hidden belongings from the same time period was a glass cosmetic container that looks somewhat like a rose vase, and a mirror of polished metal.

It occurs to me that on their annual trips to the Temple in Jerusalem it would not have been out-of-the-ordinary that Joseph may have bought his wife, Mary, some jewelry made from gold or silver, pearls or gems, or some of these glass items as a special gift. Perhaps even some imported silk. So that although they might not have been made in Nazareth, they were still easily obtainable by the Holy Family. Perhaps Mary also had a rose vase at home for the rose that grew in her garden that her son, Jesus, weeded for her, and from which he would lovingly cut a bloom for his Mother.

To protect one's head and neck from the sun they wore a piece of cloth that falls over the shoulders, held on with a cord or strip of cloth, much like we see today in the Holy Land. And, of course, they could also drape their cloak over their head, or hold it over their face in a windstorm. This cloak was really a versatile garment.

We assume that the only footwear they had was sandals, but they also had a type of shoe that they could wear in cold or rainy weather. These would have been made of camels hide for everyday use; the rich wore shoes made of jackal or hyena hide. Sandals were made of camel hide or wood, with a leather thong holding them to the foot. However, they could not wear either shoes or sandals into the synagogue or Temple.

So often we see men carrying a staff in drawings of those days. These functioned much as today's "walking sticks" and were used not only for support, but also to ward off animals, and could also be used as a weapon when one was attacked.

Speaking of drawings, the Jews did not make representations of the human form as the Egyptians did, so all of these descriptions of their clothing are the "educated guesses" of learned people. However, having represented Joseph in the "Living Nativity" at our church one year at Christmas time, and Wise Men on several other Christmas seasons, I can tell you that the clothing that we've just described is not uncomfortable. And I, for one, have no difficulty accepting these descriptions as to what our Lord and his family would have worn.

If you ever have an opportunity to "represent" one of the Holy Family at a "Living Nativity" I urge you to do so. This tradition was started by St. Francis of Assisi in 1223 A.D., and I can tell you that they have been some of the most profound religious moments of my life. You gain a great personal awareness of the Holy Family, but you also receive unbelievable blessings from the people who see you. No one can ever fully know the effect you have on their often troubled lives. We can never truly know the anguish in another's heart that may be calmed and soothed by seeing such a scene. Especially at a time of year that is often extremely sad and stressful for many people. It is a wonderful tradition that I wish all Christian Churches would emulate. It is especially moving when a teenage girl plays Mary, older men Joseph, both men and women the Wise Men, and teenage boys and girls as shepherds. And don't forget the live sheep and a donkey. They will really put you in a Biblical mood, and you will have no difficulty transporting yourself back through time to the nativity cave in Bethlehem.

Drawings by: Michael J. Lattimer

"Kohl sticks". These are thin twisted glass rods that women used during the time of Jesus to apply the black paint, called kohl, to their eyes. They were twisted and look much like long modern screws; however, they have one end rounded, the other end pointed and were about six inches long.

Sources for this chapter, and recommended reading for you:

Dr. Alfred Edersheim, *Sketches of Jewish Social Life, in the days of Christ.* Wm. B. Eerdmans Publishing Company, Grand Rapids, Michigan.

Dr. Alfred Edersheim, *The Life And Times of Jesus The Messiah.* Wm. B. Eerdmans Publishing Company, Grand Rapids, Michigan.

Nahman Avigad, *A Craft Center for Stone, Pottery, and Glass, Jerusalem Flourishing.* Biblical Archeology Review, November/December 1983, Vol. IX, No. 6. Pages 48-59.

The Lion Publishing Corporation, *The Lion Encyclopedia of the Bible.* © 1978 by Lion Publishing. Originally published by Lion Publishing plc, Icknield Way, Tring, Herts, England. Published in the United States by The Reader's Digest Association, Inc. with permission of LIon Publishing Corporation.

9

His Personal Hygiene & Health

Keeping oneself clean is always important, but especially in those distant days before our modern medicines and health care. Daniel-Rops tells us that "Washing was among the great requirements in Leviticus: 'Keep your persons undefiled.' It was literally a sin to eat without having washed one's hands. Washing thoroughly, said the rabbis, was better than all medicine. The ashes of soda-yielding plants together with some kind of fat were used for washing."

Even today, some people still make their own soap, much like it must have been done in Mary's day. They use the accumulated grease from cooking meat along with lye, obtained from ashes, to make a very useful soap. As I write this we still have some here in our home that my wife made with our beloved Aunt Lucile before she died at the age of 90. I use it whenever I need a good strong soap to get my hands really clean, or when bit by a yellow fly or mosquito to cleanse and soothe the bite.

The craftsmen in Jesus' day no doubt used a similar strong handsoap the same way at the end of their labors. No doubt a wash basin and a pitcher of water was kept by the back door of the house so that Joseph and his sons could wash up before coming in to eat. Just as is still done on some ranches and farms.

Pumice stone was also common in those days and Natron from Egypt. This soda-type material was also used by the Egyptians in embalming.

We know that they had cloth that could have been used in cleansing themselves, but in those days they also had sponges. Remember the sponge full of vinegar and water that was offered to Jesus as he hung dying on the Cross? As I write this there are five sponge boats in our small harbor here in Cedar Key on the Gulf, and Nazareth was not that far from the Mediterranean where sponges would also have been abundant. Greeks here in Florida, from nearby Tarpon Springs, as well as back in their native country really know how to find sponges.

Although they had brushes in those days, the toothbrush had not yet been invented, nor toothpaste; however, Daniel-Rops tells us that "to make one's breath pure, 'scented pepper' was used—no doubt a kind of anise."

And they had barbers and hairdressers, too, but I would suspect the common people took care of this themselves at home. The Roman men shaved their faces and slaves were not permitted to wear beards, but Jewish men, as far as can be told, wore them proudly, just as many men do today. In view of the tensions between the occupying Romans in the land and the resident Jews, I would bet that wearing a beard was an act of defiance for a great many men, and for the rest it would have been expected in silent support. It was evidently the fashion for men to let their sideburns grow into curls, just as we see today on a certain sect of Jews. And they had combs in those days made of ivory or wood, sometimes even gold for the wealthy.

Perfumes and scents were available for those who wanted them. Remember the oil that Mary Magdelene poured on Jesus' hair, and the nard she put on his feet. Although the nard scent could be made from local plants, the expensive kind came from India by caravan. The nard plant has heart-shaped leaves, small greenish-white flowers and reddish berries. The ointment, or perfume, is made from the roots of these plants. Balm was also popular, as were scents made from roses, lilies and jasmine softened in oils.

Tattoos were forbidden by Leviticus.

As far as illnesses were concerned, Daniel-Rops tells us that "the Jews in Jesus' day suffered from the common cold, pneumonia, inflammation of the lungs, dysentery *(diarrhea, abdominal pain),* eye disease due to sandstorms and dust, leprosy of many kinds and venereal diseases. Mosquitoes were also a problem, as was malaria.

The Jewish physicians and common-folk used many things for medicinal purposes. Oil was rubbed on the skin or wounds, sometimes mixed with wine. Honey also was put on open wounds and swallowed for sore throats. A poultice of figs was used for anthrax. Anthrax is a dangerous disease that people catch from sheep or cattle. They also used purple aloes mixed with wine, rosemary, hysop, rue, and bigonia. And palm barley soaked in curdled milk for heart palpitations. Maidenhair fern was used against tape-worms, and fish brine for rheumatism. They had eye salves, and practiced bleeding, cupping and primitive surgery. They also used the restorative abilities of thermal baths. They cauterized wounds, lanced abscesses and set fractures. They also performed Caesarean birth deliveries. And they pulled teeth. They used garlic for toothaches and salt or yeast for gum disease.

Some of them even wore artificial limbs."

It is not a stretch of the imagination to assume that Jesus must have had the common cold just as you and I, and suffered with it much the same way.

Sources for this chapter, and recommended reading for you:

Henri Daniel-Rops, _Daily Life in the Time of Jesus, An authentic reconstruction of Biblical Palestine and the day-to-day lives and customs of its people._ © 1962 Hawthorn Books, Inc. 70 Fifth Avenue, New York, NY 10011. Mentor-Omega Book Edition, Published by The New American Library. Originally published in France by Librairie Hachette, © 1961.

10

His Religion

It may seem presumptuous for an ordinary person to try to write about the religion that Jesus practiced when he was living among us. How difficult would it be for you today to sit down with pencil, pen or mouse and keyboard and try to explain your own religion? Could you really do it and be accurate? Is yours a faith truly of your intellectual mind or of your heart? I bet the latter is closer to the truth for most of us. I have now lived more than 3 score years and am still a beginner when it comes to this subject even though I at one time contemplated entering the religious life. Whether you attend Baptist, Roman Catholic, United Methodist, Presbyterian, Episcopal, Pentecostal, United Church of Christ, Amish, Mennonite, Disciples of Christ, Latter Day Saints, Congregational or some other branch of the Christian faith, you probably know just a portion about your own form of religion that your priest, minister, preacher or lay leader knows. We are probably no more aware of this than during sermons when our learned religious leaders preach to us from the Gospels, often from sections we are only vaguely aware of, unless we are among the few who also regularly attend Bible Study or Sunday School Classes.

Our Christian religion today is built not only on the words and life of Yeshua bar Yosef *(Jesus Christ)*, but also upon the thousands of years of Old Testament messages in what the Jews call the *Tanakh*...this is the Hebrew Bible, composed of the Torah, the Neviim and the Ketuvim. We basically use their "Bible" plus our own in practicing our Christian faith. And, obviously, Jesus used only theirs, the *Tanakh,* or rather, the first two parts of it that existed in his lifetime*.*

I have hesitated to write this chapter since I have never had a formal course in religion, other than catechism class when I was a young boy of about 10, nor have I studied anything about theology in depth, other than my own rather extensive research and reading over the years including much of the material in this book. "Curiosity of the Ordinary Person" can be a powerful motivator, can't it? So if you happen to be a religious leader, rather than the ordinary people that this small book is intended to reach, I trust you will forgive my rather simplistic approach to the subject matter. Just as you did in your seminary or bible school days I must rely on the explanations of others in order to gain a better understanding of this complex subject of how Jesus practiced his religion. And, as you will soon see in this chapter, His religion, indeed, was complex.

"Jesus *(Yeshu)* was, of course, a Jew, not a Christian." So wrote Irving Zeitlin in his book "Jesus and the Judaism of His Time". "This obvious and fundamental fact is lost sight of all too often. He was circumcised as a Jew, lived as a Jew and prayed as a Jew; he performed the Jewish rites and he preached in Aramaic to his fellow Jews in the synagogues of Palestine. All of this is related frankly and unabashedly in the Gospels. Jesus was deeply rooted in the early first-century Jewish world."

Zeitlin continues-"Jesus the pious Jew fastidiously observed the Law; he celebrated Passover *(Mark 14:12)*, taught in the Temple *(Mark 14)*, and wore *tsitsit* *(Mark 6:56)*, the fringe or tassels attached to the four corners of a robe in fulfillment of the commandment in Numbers 15:37-41 and Deuteronomy 22:12. In addition, Jesus showed due regard for the temple by paying the half shekel tax *(Matt. 17:27)*; and he acknowledged that 'the scribes and Pharisees sit on Moses seat; so practise and observe whatever they tell you' *(Matt.23:2-3)*."

In his book "The Jews in the Time of Jesus" Rabbi Stephen M. Weylan provides us with an interesting view of religion as it existed when Jesus lived. "First century Judaism consisted of 'the ways of our ancestors'—that is, doing things in the traditional way. The service of God was continuous with the agricultural and pastoral cycle of the land of Israel; the festivals and sacrificial offerings corresponded to planting and harvest and the birthing of domestic animals. The best available analogy for moderns may be the "Way" of the American Plains Indian. The religion of the Plains Indian was in no way separate from the buffalo hunt and the planting of corn and tobacco; the religion and the way of life are inconceivable without each other. Judaism also was a "Way"...The earliest Christians similarly called their religion The *Way*—the Way of Christ."

Jesus would have said the Shema *(see pages 90-91)* and the Tefillah *(Amidah, see below)* each day.

Here is what Rabbi Hayim Halevy Donin, in his book "To Pray As A Jew" tells us about the Shema:

70

"Shema Yisrael, Adonai eloheinu, Adonai ehad"
Hear O Israel, The Lord is our God, the Lord is One.

"The Shema is not a prayer in the ordinary sense of the word, but for thousands of years it has been an integral part of the prayer service. The Shema is a declaration of faith, a pledge of allegiance to One God, an affirmation of Judaism. It is the first "prayer" that children are taught to say. It is the last utterance of martyrs. It is said on arising in the morning and on going to sleep at night. It is said when one is praising God and when one is beseeching Him. The faithful Jew says it even when questioning Him. The Shema is said when our lives are full of hope; it is said when all hope is gone and the end is near. Whether in moments of joy or despair, in thankfulness or in resignation, it is the expression of Jewish conviction, the historic proclamation of Judaism's central creed."

As Rabbi Donin said, the Shema is said morning and evening and the Tefillah three times each day. Today the Tefillah contains 19 benedictions or prayers, but in Jesus' day it probably contained just 6 according to the rabbis. Pilkington tells us that the word Tefillah *(prayer)* "possibly derives from the Hebrew root for "to judge", with the thought that in Tefillah people call on God to judge all their thoughts and actions. This may include the notion of self-examination, judging oneself." The Tefillah is prayed while standing and facing Jerusalem; if done while in Jerusalem, then he would face the Temple. The Jew in Jesus' time did not fold his hands while praying as many of us do today, that was a later "invention". Rather, he would often raise his hands toward Heaven while praying aloud while in a group, or silently when alone. Here is what he would have prayed during Tefillah, as revealed to us by Alfred Edersheim:

I. "Blessed be the Lord our God and the God of our fathers, the God of Abraham, the God of Isaac, and the God of Jacob; the great, the mighty, and the terrible God; the Most High God, Who showeth mercy and kindness, Who createth all things, Who remembereth the gracious promises to the fathers, and bringeth a Saviour to their children's children, for His own Name's sake, in love. O King, Helper, Saviour, and Shield! Blessed art Thou, O Jehovah, the Shield of Abraham."

II. "Thou, O Lord, art mighty for ever; Thou, Who quickenest the dead, art mighty to save. In Thy mercy Thou preservest the living; Thou quickenest the dead; in Thine abundant pity Thou bearest up those who fall, and healest those who are diseased, and loosest those who are bound, and fulfillest Thy faithful word to those who sleep in the dust. Who is like unto Thee, Lord of strength, and

71

who can be compared to Thee, Who killest and makest alive, and causest salvation to spring forth? And faithful art Thou to give life unto the dead. Blessed be Thou, Jehovah, Who quickenest the dead!"

III. "Thou art holy, and Thy Name is holy; and the holy ones praise Thee every day. Selah! Blessed art Thou, Jehovah God, the Holy One!"

The three concluding segments were as follows: (then they would have been IV, V, and VI, today they are XVII, XVIII and XIX):

XVII. "Take gracious pleasure, O Jehovah our God, in Thy people Israel, and in their prayers. Accept the burnt-offerings of Israel, and their prayers, with Thy good pleasure; and may the services of Thy people Israel be ever acceptable unto Thee. And oh that our eyes may see it, as Thou turnest in mercy to Zion! Blessed be Thou, O Jehovah, Who restoreth His Shechinah to Zion!"

XVIII. "We praise Thee, because Thou art Jehovah our God, and the God of our fathers, for ever and ever. Thou art the Rock of our life, the Shield of our salvation, from generation to generation. We laud Thee, and declare Thy praise for our lives which are kept within Thine hand, and for our souls which are committed unto Thee, and for Thy wonders which are with us every day, and Thy wondrous deeds and Thy goodnesses, which are at all seasons—evening, morning and midday. Thou gracious One, Whose compassions never end; Thou pitying One, Whose grace never ceaseth—for ever do we put our trust in Thee! And for all this Thy name, O our King, be blessed and extoled always, for ever and ever! And all living bless Thee—Selah—and praise Thy Name in truth, O God, our Salvation and our Help. Blessed art Thou, Jehovah; They Name is the gracious One, to Whom praise is due."

XIX. "Oh bestow on Thy people Israel great peace, for ever; for Thou art King and Lord of all peace, and it is good in Thine eyes to bless Thy people Israel with praise at all times and in every hour. Blessed art Thou, Jehovah, Who blesseth His people Israel with peace."

* * * * * * *

Today there are many degrees to which people practice their faith, regardless of what basic core religion they adhere to-Judaism, Christianity, Buddhism, Islam, Confucianism, Sikhism, Taoism, Shinto, etc. Even in our own small churches out here at the 'Edge of the World' there are those who carry their Bibles each Sunday in order to follow the Bible readings, some others do not. Some read the Bibles provided in the pews, others do not. It is the same with most other facets of life. Some people are strict, precise and very conservative in their religious and life practices, others more relaxed and loose. Who does God favor more? I'll bet he loves both equally.

And so it was in Jesus' time. The Pharisees strictly followed the Oral Law passed down from generation to generation and demanded tight observance of each small detail of the Law...to the 600 sections of Jewish Law. The Sadducees had their own ideas. Ordinary people would have had a third way of looking at things, and this would often vary from family to family, just as it does with us today.

Here's what E.M. Blaiklock says about the Pharisees and Sadducees in his book "Today's Handbook of Bible Characters". "The Pharisees *(and the name appears to mean 'the Separated')*, were the leaders in *(the)* biblical revival *(following the Jewish exile)*. The Law was their incessant study...in ardor, faith and dedication they did fine work. And then, like so many who thus begin, they ended in pride and pettiness, "separated" not from paganism, evil and compromise, but from the mass of Israel, the "accursed crowd" *(John 7:49)*. The Law became, not a means to holiness, but holiness itself, a clutter of man-made regulations which they themselves could only keep by inventing, along with their detailed obligations, a parallel series of escape clauses which poisoned their practice with hypocrisy."

Of the Sadducees, Blaiklock says, "The Sadducees were a worldly sect who had cornered the prestige, the possessions and the emoluments of the priesthood. They accepted only the five books of Moses...they abandoned all belief in a resurrection and an afterlife *(Acts 23:6-10)*. Belief determines conduct. With no thought of judgment to come, the Sadducee found it easy to turn the Temple court into a sordid place of merchandise. He found no impediment to murder, when an awkward Galilean disturbed, or was thought to disturb, the relationship of compromise and collaboration which had been worked out with the occupying *(Roman)* forces. The Sadducees were ignorant as well as worldly. Learning was with the Pharisees and the scribes...it is the way of ignorant men to be supercilious in argument, and to attack by ridicule. They sought to make the teaching of Christ appear absurd, and argued with crass insincerity."

Jacob Neusner in "Judaism in the Beginning of Christianity" says "The Sadducees were most influential among landholders and merchants, the Pharisees among the middle and lower urban classes, the Essenes among the disenchanted of both these classes.

And so we see that there were wide differences, even among the "leaders" in Jerusalem of what religion should be. Imagine, then, what the common man and woman thought of all of this. I would suspect that people out in the villages tried to follow as many of the Oral Laws as possible, while still living their daily lives as smoothly as could be. Christians and Jews today have varying degrees of relating to religion in their daily lives. I see no reason to suspect that Jews in the time of Jesus were otherwise. Human nature is human nature.

Before we get into the nuances of the beauty of the Jewish religion, let us ask ourselves what a typical day in the life of Jesus would have been like as far as his practice of his religion. I base this on the work of others, but am sure he will correct me when I die if this contains deviations from what he actually did. Here is our best guess.

Rabbi Milton Steinberg in "Basic Judaism" says "This is the normal Jewish day as blocked out by the Tradition and practiced by all Jews in the past and by orthodox Jews to the present...On awakening and before he so much as stirs, a Jew thinks of his gratitude to God for life and the return of consciousness. 'I give thanks before Thee,' he prays, 'King living and eternal, that Thou has mercifully restored my soul to me; great is Thy faithfulness.'

"Then he rises, and with each act in the process of getting up recites an ordained blessing: on washing his hands and face, prescribed as his first duty; on setting foot on the ground; on attending to his bodily needs, on donning an undergarment adorned with the fringes commanded by the Torah. So he refers his every move to God and fulfills the instruction that a man shall be strong as a lion and fleet as a deer to do the will of his Father who is in Heaven."

It should be noted that women are exempt from much of this so that it does not interfere with their role as wife and mother. You may not know that being a Jew is defined as having been born of a Jewish Mother.

Rabbi Steinberg goes on—"Then he prepares for formal worship. Again he wraps himself in a fringed garment, save that this time it is the large, outer prayer-shawl worn only during religious exercises or sacred study. Next he takes up his tefilin, two little boxes encasing selected passages from Scripture, and, by means of the leather thongs with which they are equipped, ties them to himself, so fulfilling in utmost literalness the Biblical commandment: "Thou shalt bind them *(i.e., God's words)* for a sign upon thine hand, and they shall be for frontlets between thine eyes." One of these containers he fastens to his left arm, next to his heart; a symbolic commitment of heart and hand to God's will. The other he affixes to his forehead above his eyes, making a like consecration of his intellect. Finally he ties the leather thong about his left hand in a mystical knot suggestive of the divine name. With each act he recites apposite benedictions. With the last act, moreover, the entwining of the fingers, he pledges himself to God with Hosea's magnificent lines of spiritual espousal:

I will betroth thee unto Me forever;
Yea, I will betroth thee unto Me in righteousness, and in justice,
And in loving kindness, and in compassion.
And I will betroth thee unto Me in faithfulness;
And thou shalt know the Lord.

So, bound to God, wedded to His will, the Jew is ready for his morning devotions, which consist in the recitation of Psalms, in prayers, some of personal reference, others affirming the group faith and ideals of Israel, and in passages from Scripture and rabbinic literature included for purposes of religious study."

Rabbi Stephen M. Weylan, in speaking of tefilin, tells us that "To imagine the discussion in Jesus' day we must realize that tefilin in that time were flat, resembling a leather version of a kerchief worn tied around the head."

Rabbi Steinberg goes on to tell us that when the Jew is finished with these prayers, he then takes off the tefilin and can eat his breakfast. "Hands are washed and a brief benediction is spoken before bread is broken; a longer grace follows the repast. What is more, observances persist thereafter. Twice more, once in the afternoon and once again at dusk, the Jew engages in formal worship. Between times he invokes God's name frequently, since the Tradition ordains benedictions for almost every juncture of his life...food between meals...don a new garment...taste a fruit just then in season, see a flash of lightning, hear thunder, catch a glimpse of the ocean or of a rainbow or of trees burgeoning in the spring, encounter one learned in Torah or in secular lore, hear good news or be the recipient of bad—for almost every conceivable contingency there exists a brief but appropriate word of blessing."

"And at night on retiring he prays still again in gratitude for sleep, in affirmation of his faith, and in self-commitment to divine care; so that the day ends as it began, with the consciousness of God."

How many of those of us who are Christians are this faithful to our religion, or this observant of the details of practicing it on a daily basis? My own experience over the years has been that the practice of religion is a very small part of my daily life, even though for an hour each Sunday I have always embraced it warmly and deeply. Also on Sunday my wife and I participate in our Sunday School group before our weekly Worship Service, and in the evening our small Prayer Circle to pray for those in need. We also spend a moment each day praying for the people on our weekly Prayer List. Grace before meals and brief thoughts about the Lord and Holy Family are about as far as the rest of my daily practice of formal religion goes. Of course, living a life filled with a Christian spirit each day is something that we all should strive to do. But most of us come nowhere close to how the pious Jew observes his wonderful religion.

* * * * * *

Not long after Jesus died, a great event took place in nearby Sepphoris, just 4 miles from his home in Nazareth *(in about 200 A.D.)*. Rabbi Judah ha-Nasi *(Judah the Prince)*, the Patriarch of the seventy-one member Sanhedrin, compiled the Oral Law into the Mishnah. The Mishnah *(meaning Instruction)* is the collection of Jewish legal traditions and is a basic part of the Talmud. Rabbi Judah actually completed the work begun after the Romans destroyed Jerusalem in 70 A.D. It was then *(probably beginning in 160 A.D.)* that the Jews began putting their Oral Law into writing. The Talmud is composed of 63 books, the Mishnah being only one part. The second part is the Gemara, really two books *(the Palestinian and the Babylonian)*, these are scholarly comments for the Jews to follow regarding the Mishnah. The Babylonian text completed in about 500 A.D. is the most widely followed of the two. Both the Mishnah and the Gemara were written in a mixture of Hebrew and Aramaic *(Jesus' tongue)*.

According to Steven Fine, writing in Biblical Archaeology Review, "The Oral Torah was believed to provide the interpretations and explanations that make

God's written revelation applicable to life in every age. In turn, this Oral Torah is traditionally divided between law *(halakhah)* and lore *(aggadah)*. These are complimentary...H. N. Bialik, the "poet laureate" of modern Israel, has succinctly expressed the relationship between Jewish law and lore:

"Like ice and water, Halakhah and Aggadah are really two things in one, two facets of the same entity."

Eugene J. Lipman, in his book "The Mishnah, Oral Teachings of Judaism" gives us some more insight into this important body of work. "As soon as the Jewish people settled down after the first Babylonian exile which ended officially in 538 B.C.E. *(Before Common Era, i.e., before Jesus' birth, B.C., Before Christ)*, although maximum resettlement in Palestine took another century to be completed, they used scholars and scribes to make decisions in cases which arose in their communities and were not covered directly by Torah law. This process continued uninterrupted for five centuries..." "Both Aggadic Midrash and Halakhic Midrash were collected and written down during the last two pre-Christian centuries and the first century of the Common Era...By the time the Temple was destroyed in 70 C.E., the body of Halakhic discussion and decision were enormous. Most of it had not been written down. But there was great anxiety among the scholars and sages about the future of Judaism...Then the Nasi *(Sanhedrin president)* Rabbi Judah decided to compile an authoritative and "complete" corpus of Halakhah. A group of scholars set to work on the task, which continued for many years. Though we do not know exactly when they began or finished, it can be said with some certainty that the finished work-the Mishnah-was completed by 200 C.E."

The most prominent Jewish religious leader just prior to Jesus' birth was Hillel The Elder. He is thought to have lived between 70 B.C. and 10 A.D. In other words, if the date of his death is correct he would have died just a short time after Jesus astounded the elders in the Temple when he was 12 years old. Is it possible that Hillel was in the Temple that day listening to the young boy from the small village up north in Galilee? Hillel was known, according to the World Book Encyclopedia, for his "humility and for his love for his fellowman. Many of his sayings are similar to the later teachings of Jesus. Hillel described the meaning of Judaism in simple terms. He said" "What is hateful to thee, do not unto thy fellowman; this is the whole Law; the rest is mere commentary."

Hillel became a prominent spiritual leader at about the age of 40 *(30 B.C)* and became an authority on the interpretation of Biblical Law. He was a descendant of the House of David *(as was Joseph, Jesus' foster father)* and was born in Babylonia. I've heard of Babylon all my life, but must confess, I had to look it up to see where it was located. I found that it was an ancient region around the Tigris and Euphrates Rivers in Mesopotamia *(now southeastern Iraq)*. The ancient city of Babylon was 60 miles south of present day Baghdad, Iraq on the Euphrates River. Al Hillah, Iraq now stands at that site. This area is east of Israel.

"Because of his great learning," the World Book tells us, "Hillel was made a prince of the Sanhedrin, the highest Court in the Jewish State". In 30 B.C. he became President of this Court *(sort of like the Chief Justice of the U.S. Supreme Court)* and held office for 40 years. His main goal was to give greater care to the study of Jewish Law. Hillel made it easier to study *(the 600 sections of Jewish Law)* by arranging them under six headings. He also set rules for interpreting the Scripture. Hillel's chief spiritual rival was Shammai, who founded a more conservative school of interpretation. But according to Lipman's book, if I've read it correctly, most decisions nowadays follow Hillel's teachings.

An interesting thing about Babylon that I uncovered while researching this was that the Biblical word for Babylon was Babel *(the Tower of Babel)*. After the Great Flood, Noah's descendants settled here and started to build the Tower in order to reach Heaven. But God did not want that done. My interpretation is that God want's us to reach Heaven by spiritual, not physical, development. At any rate, God caused all of the people building this Tower to suddenly start talking in different languages. Since they could not then understand one another, they had to stop building. And the Hebrews believe that this was the origin of the world's various religions.

Thus the body of Jewish Law in the Mishnah came about, following God's opening the eyes and minds of many people over hundreds of years. It is important for all of us to realize that what we accomplish during our lives, as minor as it may seem to us, is really only part of the bigger Plan that God has in Mind and that he is working on for the perfection of the Universe as he brings order out of the chaos of the Creation, or the Big Bang, if you believe in that theory. You may ask, if God is truly all powerful why doesn't he just do this instantaneously. I believe that that would take away the sweetness of this Act of Creation that we are all still a part of and that is still going on when you look at the long picture. Why the need for Worlds and Creatures then? Who can look around them and not marvel and not be overwhelmed to weep at the beauty of this thing, this Universe, God has Created? Isn't it part of the wonder of it all that God has created all of this so that we all can take part in the Act of Creation of the Ultimate?

According to Lipman, here is how the Mishnah is laid out. I am deleting his use of most of the Hebrew terms, with all due respect to that religion that I hold in such high regard, simply for the sake of brevity. I trust my Jewish friends will forgive me. My goal is to make the rich Jewish Tradition more understandable to Gentiles like myself, so that they can more easily understand the religion that Jesus followed as he grew up. Our Jewish brothers and sisters of today still follow many of these Laws, and still study them. Some Jews follow them more closely than others, just as they did in Jesus' time. Incidentally, Louis Jacobs in the Oxford University Press' "Jewish Religion" tells us that "the English word "Jew" is derived from the Latin which, in turn, is based on the Hebrew word Yehudi, meaning "from the tribe of Judah" *(Judah=Yehudah)*."

The First Order:
(Seeds: The Laws of Agriculture)

Blessings
Edge of the Field
Doubtful Crops
Diverse Kinds
The Seventh Year
Heave-Offerings
Tithes
Second Tithe
Dough Offering
Fruit of the Trees
First Fruits

The Second Order:
(Festivals)

Sabbath
Sabbath Travel Regulations
Passover
Temple Taxes
The Day of Atonement
Booth

79

An Egg
New Year Observance
Fast Days
The Scroll of Esther
Mid-Festival Days
Festival Sacrifice

The Third Order:
(Women)

Sisters-in-law
Marriage Contracts
Vows
The Nazirite-vow
The Suspected Adulteress
Divorces
Marriage

The Fourth Order:
(Civil and Criminal Law)

The First Gate
The Middle Gate
The Last Gate
The High Court
Punishment by Flogging
Oaths
Testimonies
Idolatry
Erroneous Decisions

The Fifth Order:
(Sacred Things)

Animal Sacrifices
Flour Offerings
Unconsecrated Animals
First-Born
Evaluations
Exchanges of Sacrificial Cattle
Divine Punishment

Inadvertent Sacrilege
Daily Sacrifice
Measurements
Bird Offerings

**The Sixth Order
(Ritual Purity)**

Vessels
Tents
Leprosy
The Red Cow
Cleanliness
Ritual Baths
The Menstruating Woman
Prerequisites for Non-Kashrut
Bodily Discharges in Illness
Post-Immersion Uncleanliness
Uncleanliness of Hands
Stalks and Ritual Uncleanliness

Just like you and I are constantly a "work in progress", so, too, was it with the Jewish religion in the time of Jesus. How, then, did the everyday Jew live his religion? What did Jesus do? We can never know for sure what he did, but what we can do, is look at some of the existing Law outlined above that existed at the time of Jesus, and as later set down in writing in the completed Mishnah. I will leave it up to you to decide which of these examples ordinary Jews like Jesus, Mary and Joseph would have followed in their everyday lives and in their home. What would you have done, when faced with whether to follow all of these Laws, or not, in your everyday life?

Rabbi Stephen M. Wylen tells us in this regard that "The consistent point of Jesus' message is that the outward observance of the Law should be matched by an inner turning to God."

C.M. Pilkington, in speaking of the food laws, says that "This is to discipline the Jewish people towards holiness. Whatever concerns of health and hygiene may now be detected in them, the sole purpose of kashrut as stated in the Torah is to express the holiness of the covenant people."

Lipman tells us that there were four major causes of ritual defilement: death, disease, creeping things and sexual functions. "Five categories of objects are the primary causes of contamination: one who has contact with a human corpse; eight types of creeping things; dead animals; matter issuing from human skin eruptions; semen, menstrual blood; and the leper. Among the objects which can become ritually contaminated, in addition to human beings, are: clothing; metal objects; wooden vessels; skin vessels, bone vessels; earthenware; food; and drink—though food becomes contaminated only if it has first been 'prepared' by being dampened with some liquid."

I just had to open the Old Testament to read Leviticus *(11:29-30)* to see what this list of Creeping Things were. They are outlined in our Bible as:

"These are unclean for you among the creatures that swarm upon the earth: the weasel, the mouse, the great lizard according to its kind, the gecko, the land crocodile, the lizard, the sand lizard and the chameleon."

Then in Numbers *(19:11-12)* we read: "He who touches the corpse of any human being shall be unclean for seven days. They shall purify themselves with water on the third day and on the seventh day, and so be clean."

This whole matter of death is touched on by Lipman, too. When is death official? Lipman tells us that in Roman Catholic Law the soul departs the body four hours after death. But in traditional Judaism, when aspiration *(breathing)* and heartbeat stop, the soul leaves the body.

And while many kinds of vessels *(bowls, cups, dishes, serving trays)* could become ritually unclean, as noted above, we learn from Nahman Avigad, writing in the Biblical Archeology Review, that "the Mishnah tells us that stone vessels are among those objects that are not susceptible to uncleanness. Stone was simply not susceptible to ritual contamination. When a pottery vessel, on the other hand, became ritually unclean through contact with an unclean substance or object, it had to be destroyed. In contrast, a stone vessel would preserve its purity and thus its usability, even if it had come into contact with uncleanness."

For 14 years Avigad directed archaeological excavations in the Jewish Quarter of the Old City of Jerusalem. Whenever Avigad and his co-workers got to a stratum of the Second Temple Period *(the time in which Jesus lived)* in which a building was burnt by the Romans when they destroyed Jerusalem and the Temple in

70 A.D. they found a great number of stone vessels of all kinds, often still carrying traces of that 2000-year-old fire.

Some of these stone vessels were hand-carved, others done on a form of lathe. The lathe was powered when the carver pulled back and forth on a type of archery bow wrapped around a small wheel. A great number of the items Avigad and his diggers found look like modern day stone coffee cups, complete with finger handles.

The eminent Israeli archaeologist, Nahman Avigad, discovered items like this while excavating in the Old Jewish Quarter of Jerusalem. They date to the time Jesus lived in. The stone cup *(top)* was found so abundantly in nearly every house of that era that Avigad said they were as common as coffee cups of today. The divided dish *(below)* was perhaps used as a serving dish for olives and relishes, or perhaps even an individual dinner tray.

Drawings by the author's son,
Michael J. Lattimer

To show you the detail with which the Mishnah goes into in this area of Ritual Uncleanliness, here is how such a thing can occur, from Oholot 1:8. All of this is from Lipman:

"There are 248 parts in the human body: thirty in the foot, six to every toe, ten in the ankle, two in the lower leg, five in the knee, one in the thigh, three in the hip, eleven ribs, thirty parts to each hand *(six in each finger)*, two in the forearm, two in the elbow, one in the upper arm, and four in the shoulder. This totals 101 on one side of the body and 101 on the other. There are eighteen vertebrae in the spine, nine parts of the head, eight in the neck, six in the chest cavity, and five in the genitals. Each one of these parts can transmit defilement by contact, by being carried, or by being in a tent. When? Only when they have their appropriate flesh. If they do not have their appropriate flesh, they can transmit defilement by contact and by carrying, but they do not do so by being in a tent."

Niddah talks of the menstruating woman. When the menstrual period was over, the woman went to the mikveh *(ritual bath)*, was deemed ritually clean, and could resume sex relations with her husband. Intercourse was permitted only 2 weeks out of the month.

Water was used, as mentioned above, to purify both men and women. There had to be enough water to cover the body completely. The amount was fixed at forty se'ah if rainwater was the source *(100-120 gallons)*. Less could be used from a spring or fountain. No distinction was made between salt water and fresh water.

Here is some more about Ritual Purity of women from Leviticus *(12:1-8)*:
"If a woman conceives and bears a male child, she shall be ceremonially unclean seven days; as at the time of her menstruation, she shall be unclean. On the eighth day the flesh of his foreskin shall be circumcised. Her time of blood purification shall be thirty-three days; she shall not touch any holy thing, or come into the sanctuary, until the days of her purification are completed. If she bears a female child, she shall be unclean two weeks, as in her menstruation; her time of blood purification shall be sixty-six days.

When the days of her purification are completed, whether for a son or for a daughter, she shall bring to the priest at the entrance of the tent of meeting a lamb in its first year for a burnt offering. He shall offer it before the Lord, and make atonement on her behalf; then she shall be clean from her flow of blood. This is the law for her who bears a child, male or female. If she cannot afford a sheep, she shall take two turtledoves or two pigeons, one for a burnt offering and the other for a sin offering; and the priest shall make atonement on her behalf, and she shall be clean."

Mary would have done this following the birth of Jesus. After that momentous event in the cave stable, she and Joseph moved into a house in Bethlehem, and it was there that they lived when the Wise Men came to visit. And it was from there that they fled into Egypt.

Now lets talk about what the Jews thought about food during Jesus' time. The Law said that no natural food is ritually unclean when it is still attached to the Earth, except the proscribed animals, birds and fish.

Again, back to Leviticus *(11:1-23)* for the list of animals and fish that can be eaten.

* Any animal that has divided hoofs and is cleft-footed and chews the cud.

* But you cannot eat the camel, the rock badger, the hare, and the pig.

* You can eat everything in the waters that has fins and scales.

* You may eat birds, but not these: the eagle, vulture, osprey, buzzard, kite, raven, ostrich, nighthawk, sea gull, hawks, little owl, water hen, desert owl, carrion vulture, stork, heron, the hoopoe, and the bat.

* You may eat winged insects that have jointed legs above their feet with which to leap on the ground—the locust, bald locust, cricket and grasshopper.

Uktzin talks about "Stalks and Cleanliness":

"When olive leaves are pickled with the olives, the leaves remain ritually clean, for pickling them was only for appearances sake *(the leaves gave the appearance that the olives had been recently plucked, and were, therefore, fresh).*

The fibers on a cucumber and the sprouts on the end are ritually clean.

Other permitted foods are: turnips, radishes, cabbage, cauliflower, beets, garlic, wild garlic, onions and wild onions *(shallots or scallions)*, and wild lupine *(beans)*."

Lipman tells us an interesting aside. "When the Crusaders conquered Palestine, they found these wild onions growing at Ashkelon *(an ancient city along the Mediterranean in south Israel)*, which they called Ascelon. They named the onions ascelons. The "a" was dropped, and the word became scallions in English, shallots in French."

Here is another food-related law from the Mishnah. "You shall not boil a kid in it's mother's milk. It is forbidden to cook all flesh in milk except the flesh of fish and locusts. It is also forbidden to place flesh on the table with cheese, except the flesh of fish and locusts. If a man vows to abstain from flesh, he is permitted to eat the flesh of fish and locusts. A fowl may be placed on the table with cheese, but may not be eaten with it."

"If a drop of milk falls on a piece of meat cooking in a pot and there is enough milk to flavor the piece of meat, it is forbidden. If the pot is stirred, it is forbidden if there is enough milk to flavor all the contents of the pot." "Enough milk to flavor" is defined by the Rabbis as one part of milk to sixty of meat. If the bulk of the piece of meat is more than sixty times that of a drop of milk, the meat remains kosher. Kosher foods are those that are ritually correct. It is applied to food that is considered clean and wholesome. The slaughtering must be done without pain to the animal, it must be done quickly and with sharp instruments. All traces of blood must be removed by washing, soaking and salting.

Meat must also not be cooked with butter.

It was the custom to dilute wine with water before drinking it. It was also the custom to begin meals with a vegetable soaked in salt water, vinegar or oil."

Here is a Law that Mary would have followed when she baked bread. It is based upon Numbers *(15:17-21)* and is called Hallah, the Dough Offering.

"The Lord spoke to Moses, saying: Speak to the Israelite people and say to them: When you enter the land to which I am taking you and you eat of the bread of the land, you shall set some aside as a gift to the Lord, as the first yield of your baking, you shall set aside a loaf as a gift. You shall set it aside as a gift like the gift from the threshing floor. You shall make a gift to the Lord from the first yield of your baking, throughout the generations."

According to Lipman, the Torah says that the priests are entitled to a total of 24 different offerings. Hallah, the dough offering was one. "Many Jews today," he says, "can recall how their mothers took a pinch of dough before baking bread and burnt that small piece to ash, as their symbolic hallah offering."

Did Mary do the same? Did she and the other women take a loaf to their local synagogue...for the local Rabbi or Elders or tired travelers or for the homeless? For the synagogue has always been a refuge, in addition to a revered house of worship.

Five species of grain are subject to hallah—wheat, barley, spelt *(a wheat containing two light red kernels)*, oats and rye. The minimum measure of a hallah offering is one-twenty-fourth of the dough. Today's pinch is just symbolic.

Here are some more Laws as they apply to food. Orlah speaks of the Fruit of the Trees. This, too, the Jews got from Leviticus *(19:23-25)*.

"When you enter the land and plant any tree for food, you shall regard its fruit as forbidden. Three years it shall be forbidden to you, not to be eaten. In the fourth year all its fruit shall be set aside for jubilation before the Lord; and only in the fifth year may you use its fruit—that its yield to you may be increased: I the Lord am your God."

Then there was also Bikkurim-the Law of the First Fruits. This from Exodus *(23:16-19)*: "...and the feast of harvest, the first fruits of your labors, which you sow in the field; and the feast of ingathering, at the end of the year, when you gather in your labors out of the field. Three times in the year all your males shall appear before the Lord God. You shall not offer the blood of my sacrifice with leavened bread; neither shall the fat of my feast remain all night until the morning. The choicest first fruits of your land shall you bring into the house of the Lord your God."

"The men of Jesus' time took these first fruits to the Temple in Jerusalem, probably on the three festivals of Pesah *(Passover)*, Shavuot *(Pentecost)* and Sukkot *(Tabernacles)* when all the males had to appear in the Temple anyway.

It was also at these times that they brought their Terumot and Ma'aserot offerings of wine, oil and vegetables. The Bikkurim first fruit offerings included wheat, barley, grapes, figs, pomegranates, olives and dates for honey. In Israel today the Bikkurim Festival is still a major one. It takes place on Shavuot *(the Feast of Weeks, Pentecost)."*

"The Rabbis recommended that these offerings amount to anywhere from 1/40th to 1/60th of the harvest. And those who lived near Jerusalem brought fresh figs and grapes, while those from a distance, up north where Jesus lived, for example, brought dried figs and raisins. These processions were led by an ox, it's horns bedecked," Lipman tells us, "with gold, wearing an olive-wreath on its head. It would later be sacrificed as a peace offering. And a flute was played at the head of the procession until they reached the Temple Mount. When they reached the Temple Mount the Levites would sing Psalm 30: "I will extol thee, O'Lord, for Thou has raised me up, and has not suffered my enemies to rejoice over me."

The Torah detailed six festivals: Shabbat *(Sabbath)*, the three pilgrimage Festivals *(Pesah, Shavuot, Sukkot)*; the "time of the blowing of the shofar," i.e., Rosh Hashanah; and Yom Kippur.

Jewish Festivals are nature-oriented, tending to take place at full moon, at new moon, or at equinox or solstice. Season changes are celebrated: Spring *(Pesah-Passover)*, Summer *(Shavuot-Pentacost)*, and Fall *(Sukkot-Tabernacles)*. In post-Biblical times the fourth seasonal transition came to be marked by Hanukkah.

Lipman goes on to tell us that "all Sabbath Laws have as their purpose the lifting of the Jew out of the week's routine into a higher plane of existence. Each Sabbath, he receives symbolically, an additional soul, a Sabbath soul. He is free to think, to feel, to attain spiritual heights, to refresh his soul." "The Sabbath," he says, "is the greatest symbol of the spirit of Judaism...it raises the individual to his proper stature as the child and partner of God, co-Creator of the world, being 'but little lower than the angels.'"

There are three kinds of Laws regarding the Sabbath *(Shabbat)*, Lipman tells us, in the Mishnah. Observing these laws would have been what Jesus, Mary and Joseph would have been expected to do during their lives. How do you observe your Sabbath in your religion? Is it as stringent as this, or more relaxed? Here, then, are the three kinds of Laws:

1. The 39 prohibited forms of labor, with their derivatives. These prevent mixing Sabbath action with normal weekday labor.

2. Acts that are not actually labor, but not consistent with the sanctity of the Sabbath, and,

3. The handling of certain items was prohibited on the Sabbath during Jesus' time and later.

The 39 categories of prohibited work on the Sabbath are:" planting, plowing, reaping, binding sheaves, threshing, winnowing, cleaning crops, grinding, sifting, kneading, baking, shearing wool, washing, beating, or dyeing it, spinning, weaving, making 2 loops, plaiting or braiding, separating two threads, tying a knot, loosening a knot, sewing two stitches, tearing in order to sew two stitches, hunting a deer or any other animal, slaughtering or flaying or salting the deer, curing its skin, scraping it or cutting it up, writing two letters *(of the alphabet)*, erasing in order to write two letters, building, pulling down, putting out a fire, lighting a fire, striking with a hammer, and taking anything from one domain to another."

Here are some more rules about the Sabbath in Jesus' time gleaned from Lipman:

"1. A man should not go to the barber just before the time of the afternoon Tefillah unless he had already said it. *(The Tefillah are the petitionary prayers that are said standing up, they are the core of the Liturgy.)*

2. A man should not enter a bathhouse or a tannery, nor should he begin to eat a meal, or decide a lawsuit.

3. Meat and onions and eggs may not be roasted on Friday unless there is time for them to be finished before sundown. Bread may not be put into the oven when darkness has begun to fall, nor may cakes be put upon the coals unless there is time for a surface crust to form.

4. If a man put out a lamp on the Sabbath out of fear of non-Jews, or thieves, or an evil spirit, or to help a sick person go to sleep, he is not guilty of violating the Sabbath. But if he did so to spare the lamp or to save oil or the wick, he is guilty.

5. A woman may not go out with bands of wool or bands of flax or with her head-straps. She may not go out with a forehead-band or with head-bangles unless they are sewn on her headdress. Nor may she go out with a hairnet if she goes to a public place. She may not go out with a "golden city" *(a coronet with an engraving of the city of Jerusalem)*, or a necklace or nose-rings or with a ring that has no seal or with a needle that has no eye.

6. A man may not go out on the Sabbath wearing sandals shod with nails, or with a single sandal if he has no wound on his foot, or with Tefillin *(Phylacteries)* or with an amulet unless it has been prepared by an expert, or with a breastplate, helmet or greaves.

7. A man may not go out on the Sabbath with a sword or a bow or a shield or a club or a spear.

8. All sacred books may be saved from burning whether they are read on the Sabbath or not.

9. If a non-Jew lights a lamp on the Sabbath, a Jew may make use of the light. But if he lights it for the sake of the Jew, it is forbidden. If a non-Jew fills a trough with water for his cattle, a Jew may water his own cattle afterwards. But if the non-Jew does it for the Jew, it is forbidden.

10. One does not deliver the young of cattle on a Festival Day, but help may be given to the mother. But one does deliver a woman on Sabbath, and one may summon a midwife for her from any place. The Sabbath may be profaned for the mother's sake by tying up the umbilical cord. They may also cut it. In rabbinic law...human life and danger to life supersede the Sabbath.

11. No one may travel more than 2,000 cubits from his domicile. Certain objects cannot be carried more than 4 cubits from one's private domain." *(A cubit is the measurement of the forearm from the elbow to the tip of the middle finger, usually equal to 18 inches.)*

Now let us speak some more about prayer.

The following three prayers, the Shema, were recited twice a day, in the morning and in the evening by conscientious Jews, when Jesus lived:

"Hear, O Israel! The Lord is our God, the Lord alone. You must love the Lord your God with all your heart and with all your soul and with all your might. Take to heart these words with which I charge you this day. Impress them upon your children. Recite them when you stay at home and when you are away, when you lie down and when you get up. Bind them as a sign on your hand and let them serve as a symbol on your forehead, inscribe them on the doorposts of your house and on your gates." *(Deuteronomy 6:4-9)*

"And it shall come to pass, if ye shall hearken diligently unto my commandments which I command you this day, to love the Lord your God, and to serve him with all your heart and with all your soul, that I will give you the rain of your land in his due season, the first rain and the latter rain, that thou mayest gather in thy corn, and thy wine, and thine oil. And I will send grass in thy fields for thy cattle, that thou mayest eat and be full. Take heed to yourselves, that your heart be not deceived, and ye turn aside, and serve other gods, and worship them; and then the Lord's wrath be kindled against you, and be shut up the heaven, that there be no rain, and that the land yield not her fruit; and lest ye perish quickly from off the good land which the Lord giveth you. Therefore shall ye lay up these my words in your heart and in your soul, and bind them for a sign upon your hand, that they may be as frontlets between your eyes. And ye shall teach them your children, speaking of them when thou sittest in thine house, and when thou walkest by the way, when thou liest down, and when thou risest up. And thou shalt write them upon the door posts of thine house, and upon they gates: that your days may be multiplied, and the days of your children, in the land which the Lord sware unto your fathers to give them, as the days of heaven upon the earth." *(Deuteronomy 11:13-21)*

"And the Lord spake unto Moses, saying, Speak unto the children of Israel, and bid them that they make them fringes in the borders of their garments throughout their generations, and that they put upon the fringe of the borders a ribband of blue" And it shall be unto you for a fringe, that ye may look upon it, and remember all the commandments of the Lord, and do them; and that ye seek not after your own heart and your own eyes, after which ye use to go a whoring: That ye may remember, and do all my commandments, and be holy unto your God. I am the Lord your God, which brought you out of the land of Egypt, to be your God: I am the Lord your God." *(Numbers 15:37-41)*

These prayers were said in the direction of Jerusalem, that would have been to the south from where Jesus lived in Nazareth. "The Shema could be said in any language," Lipman tells us, "Hebrew, Aramaic, etc., but the Tefillah had to be said in Hebrew when praying alone, but could be said in any language when praying in a congregation. When praying with others, according to the rabbis, ones prayers go straight to God who understands all languages. But when a person prays alone he or she needs the "intervention of angels to persuade God to listen" to his or her prayers. Consequently, the prayer must be said in Hebrew."

"If a man recites the Shema so softly that he himself cannot hear, he has nevertheless fulfilled the mitzvah *(an act of obedience to God's command)*. Vocalizing is not essential, comprehension is."

Craftsmen like Jesus and Joseph could recite the Shema on the top of a tree or on top of a stone wall, which they may not do when they say the Tefillah. They must recite those standing up.

"A bridegroom is exempt from the mitzvah of reciting the Shema on the first night of the marriage or until the end of the next Sabbath if he has not consummated the marriage before then *(a total of four nights, since virgins were traditionally married on Wednesdays.)*

Women, slaves and minors are exempt from reciting the Shema and from putting on phylacteries *(small square leather boxes containing slips inscribed with scriptural passages from the Torah that are traditionally worn on the left arm and on the head by Jewish men during morning weekday prayers.)* But they *(women, slaves and minors)* are obliged to say the Tefillah, to perform the mitzvah of affixing and kissing a mezuzah and to say the blessings after meals."

Here are instructions for praying over certain kinds of food:

"Over the fruit of trees, one says: Praised be Thou who creates the fruit of the tree. Wine is the exception. Over wine one says: Praised be Thou who creates the fruit of the vine. Over the fruits of the earth, one says: Praise be Thou who creates the fruit of the ground. Bread is the exception. Over bread one says: Praised be Thou who brings forth bread from the earth. Over vegetables, one says: Praised be Thou who creates the fruit of the ground."

"When three or more persons eat together the blessings after the meal are said as a group. *(Women, non-Hebrew slaves, or minors do not count to reach the level of 3).* To be included in the group, a man must eat at least one olive, or the equivalent amount."

Here are some more rules from the Mishnah. This section is known as Pe'ah, and is based upon Leviticus 19:9-10.

"When you reap the harvest of your land, you shall not reap all the way to the edges of your field, or gather the gleanings of your harvest. You shall not pick your vineyard bare, or gather the fallen fruit of your vineyard; you shall leave them for the poor and the stranger: I the Lord am your God."

Lipman tells us that "Pe'ah should be no less than one-sixtieth of the harvest." And that "The poor may make three searches for Pe'ah each day, in the morning, at noon, and just before sunset." He quotes Rabbi Ovadya of Bertinora *(1400's)* as saying: "Early in the morning for nursing mothers, since the infants take a morning nap; at noon for youngsters, 'whole way it is to go out then', late after-noon, just before sunset, for the elderly, who walk slowly and cannot reach distant fields until late afternoon."

Gleanings are those that drop down at the moment of reaping.

Kila'yim *(Diverse Kinds)* is based upon Leviticus 19:19.

"You shall not let your cattle mate with a different kind; you shall not sow your field with two kinds of seeds; you shall not put on cloth from a mixture of two kinds of material."

"If a man wants to lay out his field in plots, each containing a different kind of crop, the school of Shammai says: Between each kind he must leave a space equal to three furrows of plowed land *(then each section can be consid-ered a separate field, with no danger of Kila'yim)*. The school of Hillel says: the width of a Sharon yoke *(approximately one yard)*. The opinion of one is close to the opinion of the other."

Kila'yim 8:2 tells us that "it is forbidden to plow or draw with them, or drive them-one kind of cattle with another, one kind of wild animal with another, cattle with a wild animal, a wild animal with cattle, one kind of non-kosher animal with another, one kind of kosher animal with another, a non-kosher animal with a kosher, a kosher animal with a non-kosher.

Shevi'it talks to us about the Seventh Year. Here are some reasons given for this "Sabbath of the Soil" Law. The number seven is a special number because of the seven days of Creation. Also, the land required a rest for its renewal. And these laws promoted God's mastery and man's dependency.

Exodus 23:10-ll tells us: "Six years you shall sow your land and gather in its yield; but in the seventh you shall let it rest and lie fallow. Let the needy among your people eat of it, and what they leave let the wild beasts eat. You shall do the same with your vineyards and your olive groves."

In closing this chapter on the Jewish Religion practiced in Jesus' time, it is important to understand and appreciate some important points made by Rabbi Stephen M. Wylen in "The Jews in the Time of Jesus".

"There is, in fact, a period of many centuries between the end of the Hebrew scriptures and the beginning of the New Testament—roughly five to seven hundred years. This period, formally called the "Intertestamental Period," is precisely the Second Temple era in which we are interested...it was a time of great religious development and change within Judaism....the last biblical book written is the book of Daniel, written about 169 BCE" *(Before Common Era, B.C. to Christians).* For some reason, Jews decided that biblical writing had come to an end with the Maccabean revolt. The council of rabbis closed the Bible for good about 100 CE, a generation after the time of Jesus...The book of Esther may have slipped into the Bible later, but basically the Bible was now closed. More than a century later the Christians added the New Testament to the scriptures. Jews, at the same time, added the Mishnah."

"In Jesus' time the Hebrew Bible contained only two of its eventual three sections—the Torah and the Prophets. These were not considered a "Bible", a single book, but two separate collections of sacred scriptures. Thus the New Testament term for sacred scripture is "the Torah *(or, Law)* and the Prophets." The closing of the Bible in the second century completed the third section, the Writings. *(Some Christians include a fourth section, the Apocrypha, in the Hebrew scriptures.)* By Jesus' time Jews had generated a great body of interpretation on how to live by these holy books. The complete "Bible" that Jesus knew consisted of not just the Torah and the Prophets, but also five hundred years worth of interpretation by Jewish sages."

Some historians, Wylen tells us, perceive Judaism and Christianity as "a mother and daughter". Others, he says "see rabbinical Judaism and Christianity as two common outgrowths of the earlier first century Judaism, each adopting different aspects of the ancient religion. To these scholars, rabbinic Judaism and Christianity are two daughters of a single mother, biblical Judaism. Judaism and Christianity are sisters."

Sources for this chapter, and recommended reading for you:

Eugene J. Lipman, *THE MISHNAH-Oral Teachings of Judaism.* © 1970 by the B'nai B'rith Commission on Adult Jewish Education. The Viking Press, Inc. 625 Madison Avenue, New York, NY 10022.

Professor Jacob Neusner, *The Mishnah: An Introduction.* © 1989 by Jacob Neusner. Published by Jason Aronson, Inc. 230 Livingston Street, Northvale, New Jersey 07647.

Professor Jacob Neusner, *JUDAISM in the Beginning of CHRISTIANITY.* © 1984 BY Fortress Press. Philadelphia, PA.

Rabbi Milton Steinberg, *Basic Judaism.* © 1947 by Milton Steinberg, © renewed 1975 by David Joel Steinberg and Jonathan Steinberg. Harcourt Brace & Company, 6277 Sea Harbor Drive, Orlando, Florida 32877-6777.

C.M. Pilkington, *Judaism.* © 1995 C.M. Pilkington. "Teach Yourself Books" NTC Publishing Group, 4255 West Touhy Avenue, Lincolnwood (Chicago), Illinois 60646. The "Teach Yourself" name and logo are registered trade marks of Hodder & Stoughton Ltd. in the UK.

Rabbi Louis Jacobs, *Concise Companion to the Jewish Religion.* © Louis Jacobs. Oxford University Press, Great Clarendon Street, Oxford OX2 6DP England.

Professor Irving M. Zeitlin, *Jesus and the Judaism of His Time.* © Irving M. Zeitlin 1988. First published 1988 by Polity Press in association with Blackwell Publishers. Reprinted 1989, 1994. Editorial Office: Polity Press, 65 Bridge Street, Cambridge CB2 1UR, UK. Blackwell Publishers, 108 Cowley Road, Oxford OX4 1JF, UK & 238 Main Street, Cambridge, MA 02142, USA.

Rabbi Stephen M. Wylen, *The Jews in the Time of Jesus.* © 1996 By Stephen M. Wylen. Paulist Press, 997 Macarthur Boulevard, Mahwah, NJ 07430.

Rabbi Hayim Halevy Donin, *To Pray as a Jew, A Guide to the Prayer Book and the Synagogue Service.* © 1980 by Hayim Halevy Donin. Published by BasicBooks, a subsidiary of Perseus Books, L.L.C.

Professor Jacob Neusner, *Judaism in the Beginning of Christianity.* © 1984 by Fortress Press. Philadelphia, PA.

Professor E.M. Blaiklock, *Today's Handbook of Bible Characters.* © 1979 E.M. Blaiklock. Published by Bethany House Publishers, a Division of Bethany Fellowship, Inc., 6820 Auto Club Road, Minneapolis, MN 55438.

The World Book Encyclopedia, © 1971 by Field Enterprises Educational Corporation.

Nahman Avigad, *A Craft Center for Stone, Pottery, and Glass, Jerusalem Flourishing.* Biblical Archeology Review, November/December 1983, Vol. IX, No. 6. Pages 48-59.

Dr. Ann Killebrew and Dr. Steven Fine, *Qatzrin, Reconstructing Village LIfe In Talmudic Times.* Biblical Archeology Review, May/June 1991, Vol. 17, No. 3. Pages 44-56.

His Apostles

It is clear to me that Jesus chose his Apostles (from the Greek word "to send") primarily from among his relatives and friends just as I probably would have done. People he knew he could trust, and who he knew were common ordinary people like you and me who could relate to the people he wanted to reach...ordinary sinners, again, just like you and me. These were not learned men who could argue the finer points of theology and discuss the obscure points of the Torah, but they tried to live their religion every day, and they tried to serve their God and their fellow man, while earning their living, as best they could.

God could have chosen to come to Earth as an earthly King and could have selected His emissaries from among the learned theologians of the day. But He did not. He knew that in order to be able to relate to the ordinary people who make up the vast majority of those living on His blue planet that He should come as an ordinary person, and choose ordinary people to carry His message. Too often today, I fear that some leaders of the world's Christian denominations forget this simple truth. They do this in both their actions and in their messages.

At least four of the 12 Apostles were relatives of Jesus, while a fifth is said to have been a member of his immediate family, but little more is known about him.

Much of what follows about the Apostles is in a fascinating book by C. Bernard Ruffin titled "The Twelve-The Lives of the Apostles After Calvary" available from Our Sunday Visitor in Huntington, Indiana. This was the latest and most concise source I could locate on the subject, although others I located are also listed at the end of this chapter.

James The Great (Big Jim, as I like to think of him) and John were brothers to one another and cousins to Jesus. Their mother, Salome, was the sister of the Virgin Mary (Miriam of Sepphoris). Their father was Zebedee. So Jesus' mother was their Aunt Mary. Her husband, their Uncle Joseph. James was a year or two older than John. Both of them were fishermen. They were to become members of Jesus' "Inner Circle" that also included Simon (Peter), who along with his brother Andrew, were partners of James and John in the highly competitive fishing business. The first century historian, Flavius Josephus, born in 37 A.D. tells us that competition was tough, indeed, for the fishermen of Jesus' day. According to him there were then 230 fishing boats plying the Sea of Galilee, the lake that is only 13 miles long by 7 miles wide.

Another set of brothers were also cousins to Jesus. They were Matthew and James The Less (Little Jim). Their father, Alphaeus, was Joseph's brother. Their mother's name was also Mary. Joseph was their Uncle, and Jesus their cousin, but if we believe in the Virgin Birth, as I do, then they would not have been related by blood to Jesus, just by marriage. Matthew and James also had two other brothers by the name of Joses and Simeon. Matthew was probably about two years older than his brother James. Both Matthew and James were civil servants, you will remember Matthew as Levi, the tax collector. Matthew reportedly was a vegetarian who lived on nuts, seeds and vegetables.

Thomas is the big question mark. The Acts of Thomas written about 200 A.D. say that Thomas was a member of Jesus' immediate family, but gives no additional information, only that he, too, was a carpenter.

As mentioned above, although not related to Jesus, there were another pair of brothers among the 12 who he must have known quite well before he invited them to join his work. They were Peter (Simon) and Andrew. Peter was the older brother by about 6 or 7 years. Their father's name was Jonah, their mother Joanna. Both Peter and Andrew were also fishermen, and as we said, they were close friends and business associates of James and John, Jesus' cousins on his Mother's side. Peter was 5 feet, 4 inches tall, a bit taller than the average man of his day. Jesus is thought to have been about 5 feet, 1 inch tall. Peter signed his name Simon bar Jonah. And it is thought that he had a fair complexion, curly hair and a short curly beard. He was stocky and muscular, no doubt from hauling in the heavy fishing nets every night upon the lake. Ruffin tells us that when Jesus met Simon he told him that henceforth his name would be "Cephas", a Greek transliteration of an Aramaic word that means "Rock". "Petros," from which we get the English "Peter," is a translation."

Two other Apostles, although not blood brothers, died together and should be mentioned together. They were the other Simon and Jude Thaddeus. Not a great deal is known about either of them. But St. Jude has long been known as the "Saint of Hopeless Causes". His given name was Judah, probably the most common name for a boy at the time.

Two other fishermen who were among the twelve were Philip and Nathanael (Bartholomew).

And the 12th Apostle was another Judah, known as Judas Iscariot. He was a Judean from the area south of Galilee, probably the only one of the twelve who was not a Galilean. He was also the treasurer for the Apostles, and would eventually embezzle their money. Judas also sold out his friend, Jesus, for 30 pieces of silver, worth about $1,200 in today's money.

Five of the twelve were originally from the fishing village of Bethsaida, at the north end of the Sea of Galilee-Peter, Andrew, James (The Great), John and Philip. Two were from Capernaum, also on the northern shore of the Sea-Matthew and James (The Less). Nathanael was from Cana where Jesus performed his first public miracle, and Judas from Kelioth in Judaea. No one knows where the other three were from. By the time Jesus reached the age of his ministry, Peter and his wife and family had also moved westward around the lake to Capernaum. Perhaps that was where Peter's wife was originally from since his mother-in-law then lived with them.

The fact that Jesus chose 12 Apostles is likely linked to Jacob's 12 sons who gave their names to the 12 tribes of Israel. Even after Judas betrayed Jesus and committed suicide, the other 11 Apostles replaced him in order to keep the number at 12. They considered Joseph Barsabbas Justus and Matthias, according to Ruffin. "The Eleven prayed, 'O Lord, you read the hearts of men. Make known to us which of these two you choose for this apostolic ministry, replacing Judas, who deserted the cause and went the way he was destined to go.' (Acts 1:24-25) They drew lots and its was Matthias who was chosen."

As we learned earlier, since this part of Palestine was so far north of Jerusalem and had such a large non-Jewish (gentile, pagan) population, all of these men no doubt spoke some Greek along with their native Aramaic, and perhaps even knew some Latin.

Matthew and John were the only two of the 12 that most likely died from natural causes. Matthew at age 90, John at the age of 97. Matthew had done the work of the Lord in Palestine, Iran and probably Egypt and Ethiopia. John did his evangelism in Palestine and Asia Minor.

Ruffin tells us that four of the Apostles were crucified. Peter at age 70 on June 29, 67 A.D. in Rome. He had carried the word of Jesus throughout Palestine, Syria, Asia Minor and into Rome itself. When faced with crucifixion, Peter asked to be crucified upside-down, perhaps feeling himself unworthy of being crucified as his Lord, Jesus, had been. His remains today are in St. Peter's Basilica in Rome.

His brother, Andrew, was also crucified. It was November 30, 69 A.D. along the shore of the Gulf of Patrae in Greece. The local governor, angered that Andrew had cured and converted his wife, and also converted his own brother, ordered that he be crucified without nails. Rather, he was tied to a cross and left to die a slow, lingering death. Rather than being torn to shreds by wild dogs, as the governor hoped, Andrew was surrounded by huge crowds of people day and night and protected. He talked to the people about God as he hung on his cross and according to legend, converted 2,000 of them to Christ before he died at the age of about 65. Andrew had journeyed throughout Palestine, Asia Minor, Scythia and Greece spreading the word of Jesus and his Resurrection during his lifetime.

Philip was crucified in 90 A.D. at the age of 87 in Asia Minor. He had angered the local Roman Governor by curing the eye disease that the man's wife suffered from, and like Peter, he, too, was crucified upside-down. At the time he was a widower with four daughters, who were also active in the early Church. They were Hermione, Chariline, Irais and Eutychiane. Hermione was also known as a healer.

Nathanael, also called Bartholomew, was flayed and crucified on August 24, 62 A.D. at about the age of 57. He had taken the Word to Palestine, Asia Minor, Armenia and even as far as central India. He has been described as being a few inches over 5 feet tall, with a fair complexion, black curly hair and a gray beard. He was also known as a friendly, cheerful man. He had journeyed to India carrying a copy of the Gospel written by Matthew. He angered the local King by converting the King's brother, the Governor, and hundreds of others and was beaten with clubs, skinned alive, then crucified, and finally beheaded near what today is Bombay, India.

James the Great (Big Jim), John's brother, was the youngest killed at the age of 40 in the year 43 A.D. He had evangelized in Palestine and some think he journeyed as far away as Spain. He was beheaded in Jerusalem at the order of King Herod for teaching that Christ was God. His relics (bones) were later taken to Spain where they are today in the Cathedral of St. James of Compostela.

James the Less (Little Jim), remained in Jerusalem and was probably stoned to death at the age of about 60 in the year 62 A.D. during a vicious persecution of Christians by the Jews.

Thomas died of stab wounds on July 3, 72 A.D. in his late 60's. This former carpenter had preached in Palestine, Osroene, Armenia, Egypt, India and Burma. Even the Hindus considered him a "Holy Man"; however some of their priests worried that Christianity would overshadow Hinduism and they attacked Thomas as he knelt praying in a cave near his home. They stabbed him with a spear and he later died in a small chapel that he had struggled and crawled to reach as he was mortally wounded.

As mentioned earlier, Simon and Jude Thaddeus died together in the year 79 A.D. Both were probably in their 70's at the time. Simon had traveled throughout Palestine, Egypt, North Africa, Britain and Iran. And Jude through Palestine, Osroene, Armenia and Iran. Simon and Jude joined forces and reportedly made 60,000 converts to Christianity in the area of Babylon. But they angered some witch doctors who turned a mob against them. Jude supposedly turned to Simon and said "I see that the Lord is calling us." They were then stoned, Jude was run through with a spear and Simon was sawn into pieces. The Roman Catholics, Lutherans and Anglicans all celebrate their lives on a joint feast day.

And, of course, Judas Iscariot hung himself.

The Apostles

C. Bernard Ruffin's Summary Chart
Reprinted with Permission from "The Twelve"
(The Author has added the relationship to Christ line)

Given Name:	Simon	Andrew	Simon	Jude
Patronymic	bar Jonah	bar Jonah	?	bar Jacob
Surname	Peter (Cephas)		Quananaya	Thaddeus
Place of Birth	Bethsaida	Bethsaida	?	?
Year of Birth	Circa 4 B.C.	Circa A.D. 5	?	?
Related to Jesus	No	No	No	No
Married	Yes	No	?	?
Occupation	Fisherman	Fisherman	?	?
Evangelism Area	Palestine, Syria, Asia Minor, Rome	Palestine Asia Minor, Scythia, Greece	Palestine Egypt, North Africa, Iran, Britain	Palestine Osroene, Armenia, Iran
Date of Death	June 29, A.D. 67	Nov. 30, A.D. 69	A.D. 79	A.D. 79
Age at Death	About 70	About 65	70's?	70's?
Manner of Death	Crucifixion	Crucifixion	Mutilation	Impaled

Given Name:	Judas	Jude	Levi	James The Less
Patronymic	bar Simon	?	bar Chalpai	bar Chalpai
Surname	Iscariot	Thomas	Matthew	
Place of Birth	Kelioth, Judaea	?	Capernaum?	Capernaum?
Year of Birth	?	?	?	?
Related to Jesus	No	Yes	Cousin	Cousin
Married	?	No ?	?	?
Occupation	?	Carpenter	Civil Servant	Civil Serv.
Evangelism Area		Palestine, Osroene, Armenia, Egypt, India, Burma	Palestine Egypt? Ethiopia? Iran	Palestine
Date of Death	A.D. 32	July 3, A.D. 72	Circa A.D. 90	A.D. 62?
Age at Death	30's ?	Probably Late 60's	About 90	About 60
Manner of Death	Suicide by Hanging	Stab Wounds	Probably Natural Death	Stoning

Given Name	James	John	Philip	Nathanael
	The Great			
Patronymic	bar Zebedee	bar Zebedee	?	bar Tolmai
	Boanergos	Boanergos		Bartholomew
Surname				
Place of Birth	Bethsaida	Bethsaida	Bethsaida	Cana
Year of Birth	Circa A.D.1	A.D. 3	Circa A.D. 3	Circa A.D.5
Related to Jesus	Cousin	Cousin	No	No
Married	No?	No	Yes	No?
Occupation	Fisherman	Fisherman	Fisherman	Fisherman
Evangelism Area	Palestine	Palestine	Palestine	Palestine,
	Spain?	Asia Minor	North Africa,	Asia Minor
			Asia Minor	Armenia,
				Central
				India
Date of Death	A.D. 43	A.D. 100	Circa A.D.90	Aug. 24,
				A.D. 62
Age at Death	Early 40's	97	87	About 57
Manner of Death	Decapitation	Natural	Crucifixion	Flaying &
		Death		Crucifixion

Sources for this chapter, and recommended reading for you:

Dr. C. Bernard Ruffin, THE TWELVE, The lives of the Apostles After Calvary, © 1984 Our Sunday Visitor, Inc., 200 Noll Plaza, Huntington, Indiana 46750.

Dr. Samuel Tilden Habel, The Twelve Apostles, A Study of Twelve Extraordinary Men Who, by Successfully Completing Their Amazing Mission, Changed the Course of History. © 1956 by Samuel Tilden Habel. Published by Creighton's Restaurant Corporation, Ft. Lauderdale, Florida.

Dr. Emil G. Kraeling, The Disciples. © 1966 by Rand McNally & Company.

Dr. William Barclay, The Master's Men. Ordinary Humans Made Great by the Transforming Power of Christ. © 1959 by William Barclay. Published by Pillar Books for Abingdon Press.

Alice Parmelee, They Beheld His Glory, Stories of the Men and Women Who Knew Jesus. © 1967 by Alice Parmelee. Published by Harper & Row, Inc. 49 East 33rd Street, New York, NY 10016.

Professor Floyd V. Filson, Pioneers of the Primitive Church. © 1940 by Floyd V. Filson. Published by the Abingdon Press

His Face

Have you ever wondered what Jesus would look like if he lived today? How would he dress if he lived in your community? What would the length of his hair be? Would he wear 4 ear piercings, have a tattoo, a nose ring? Or would he be totally straight? Would you take a second look at him if you passed him on the street? Remember, he hung out with sinners...even tax collectors and prostitutes. Wasn't Jesus really the hippie of his day? He went against the establishment, you know. Are you afraid to work with those who have AIDS, with those who drag in each day dirty and hungry into the homeless shelters and soup kitchens of your county? Those who are on welfare because of circumstances, not because it is their first choice? If they smell bad or look ragged, do you look the other way? Do you try to ignore battered women, troubled children, pregnant teenagers? Do you look the other way, rather than smile at a child with Down's Syndrome? Do you help people only of your own race or religion? Jesus didn't. He engaged with all of these kinds of people. Remember the Samaritan? He healed them, he gave them comfort. He gave them hope. He loved them. Can you ever really be sure that the dirty homeless person in front of you, or the one suffering from AIDS, isn't really Jesus come to Earth again just to test you? Mother Teresa saw Jesus in everyone she touched. So should we.

No one living today, nor for almost two-millennia, knows what Jesus looked like. We can guess, and artists have tried over the past 2,000 years to paint their version of his likeness. But what he really looked like, the timbre of his voice, what his writing looked like, what his laugh sounded like, or his anger, or his weeping, we do not know. What did he look like as he strode down those dusty roads in his sandals, his hair blowing in the breeze as he went to the next town to preach? We can only guess. Perhaps that is the way it was meant to be. God chose to come to earth at that moment in time. If he were to have come to earth at this moment in time, we would have film and video, digital cameras, DVD's, stereo-sound and three dimensional records of Jesus and his presence. But then that would not leave anything to our imagination, and it would not enable us to make Jesus look and sound like what we want him to look and sound like in order for us individually to identify with him. This way we cannot hate him, or reject him, because of the pimple upon the end of his nose. Jesus can look like us in our minds this way.

Perhaps that is another one of the great mysteries of the Creator and another of his secrets of success. He leaves things like this up to his creatures to interpret in their own way in order that they might identify more closely with him. Remember, God created us in his own likeness. And we are diverse, multi-colored, multi-talented and many. Who knows, but that when you meet God, he will reflect the color of your own skin? Or that his visage shall be like a rainbow. Perhaps when you stand before God, it will be yourself looking back at you in judgement.

So if you are Black, your Jesus can be Black. So can your God.

If Yellow, he can be Yellow.

If Copper, he can be that hue.

If Brown, Tan, Red, Pink, or White. Your Jesus can look and sound just like you. Just like you sound in your heart.

A study at Florida Atlantic University suggested that all of us on Earth today are no more distantly related than fiftieth cousins, and that most of us are a great deal closer than that. We are family.

Whatever the color your Jesus is, think of him with a gentle smile on his face and a lilting laugh upon his lips. Fear him not. Love him as he loves you. He is your brother.

His Jerusalem

Nazareth, where Jesus grew up, sits at an elevation of 1,150 feet above sea level, Jerusalem at 2,428. So when Jesus "went up" to Jerusalem, that is exactly what occurred, both figuratively and spiritually, even though Jerusalem lies 80 miles or so to the south of Jesus' home nestled in the hills of Galilee.

Yerushalayim (Jerusalem) is usually interpreted to mean "City of Peace". Many think it is the ancient Salem. Henri Daniel-Rops tells us "According to the Psalmist, the holy city must have been called Salem; for he says 'There in Salem He makes His abode, dwells in Zion' (III Kings 11:4). That, in any case is the name by which it is called in Genesis (Gen. 14:18), in that strange passage where Melchizedek, 'the king of Salem and priest of the most high God,' brings Abraham bread and wine and blesses him. Even before the days of the patriarch the true God must have been known there. The rabbinical explanation for the change in the city's name is this: well before the birth of Abraham, Shem, the son of Noah, had already called it Salem, perhaps because this word means "safety"; but the patriarch wanted to call it Jeru or Jireh, and Yahweh, so as to disappoint neither the one nor the other, cried 'Then I shall give it both names!' "By the time of Christ...Jerusalem had been the holy center of God's people for ten centuries."

Alfred Edersheim tells us that the Jerusalemites preferred to write its name Jerushalaimah.

Daniel-Rops reveals something about the topography of Jerusalem: "At the point where the city was built, the central chain of the Palestinian mountains resolves itself into a kind of plateau, which stands at an altitude of some 2,500 feet and which has been cut by the erosion of violent torrents into two raised parts running from north to the south-south-east and separated by a shallow valley that was called the Valley of the Cheesemakers, the 'Tyropoeon.' It was on the southern part of these that Jerusalem was built, a citadel protected by the deep ravine of Hinnom on the west and that of the Kidron on the east, both wadies, seasonal streams, which were often dry, but which turned into furious torrents when they were swelled by the winter floods-so furious that one of them was called 'the cloudy stream.' The western hill, which reaches 2,580 feet, is made up of the Gareb and of what the Christians have called the district of Zion: this is not the Zion of the Hebrews, but the upper town, where the wealthy had their palaces. The narrower eastern hill is divided into three smaller plateaus, the highest (2,581 feet) was called the Moriah, and upon it, covering it completely, stood the Temple. The two lower plains, which stood one to the north and the other to the south, were called Bezetha (2,411 feet) and Ophel (2,132 feet)...On the other side of the ravine of the Kidron rises a long hill whose name speaks to every Christian heart: it is the Mount of Olives, where the risen Christ vanished from his disciple's sight. Its continuation towards the south is called the Mount of Scandal, because it was there that Solomon, Solomon himself, the anointed of the Lord, permitted altars to be set up to the gods of his heathen wives. At the end of this hill, the three valleys of Jerusalem join one another to form the Wad En-Nar, whose bed runs down towards the Dead Sea."

"It was the custom of the Galileans at the time of a festival to pass through the Samaritan territory on their way to the Holy City," the historian of that day, Josephus, wrote. The Reader's Digest "Atlas of the Bible" tells us that "he (Josephus) is therein identifying the direct route that entered the hills of Samaria at Ginae and, winding its way southward past Mount Gerizim, came up to Jerusalem by the ancient north-south ridge route. Yet direct as this route was, it was often avoided by the Jews, so great was the enmity between Jew and Samaritan. Only a few years after the time of Jesus, the inhabitants of Ginae fought with Jewish pilgrims from Galilee, killing a number of them. This was an outbreak of the deep hatreds that existed in the land and had added to the dangers along the roads as Jesus went back and forth between Galilee and Jerusalem."

"The Gospel of John reports that Jesus was in Jerusalem on at least five occasions during the years of his ministry. According to John, Jesus went up to Jerusalem for Passover soon after the call of his first disciples and the miracle at Cana. Perhaps he traveled the central ridge route."

"On his return to Galilee, Jesus would most likely have retraced his path through the heart of Samaria. As he walked along the broad, hot (it was in the springtime) valley floor north of the Ascent of Lebonah, he saw the low-lying hills to the east and the gradually rising heights to the west. Then Mount Gerizim came into view. Passing under its heights, he came to Sychar, near the ruins of ancient Shechem. Where two important routes came together by Jacob's Well he sat down, weary from his journey. When a woman of Samaria came to draw water from the well, Jesus talked with her. Pointing out the rugged crags of Mount Gerizim towering above them, she said, 'Our fathers worshiped on this mountain; and you say that in Jerusalem is the place where men ought to worship.' Looking beyond both the sacredness of Mount Gerizim to the Samaritans, where their temple had stood, and the sacredness of the Temple in Jerusalem to the Jews, Jesus replied, 'true worshipers will worship the Father in spirit and truth..."

Jesus might also have walked down the Jordan River valley from Capernaum to Jericho and then turned west through the Wilderness of Judea to reach Jerusalem on some of his visits.

As the land bridge between Africa, Asia and Europe, Israel's history goes back at least a million years to the time that mankind first moved out of the cradle in Africa and started to spread over the globe. Archaeologists estimate that Jerusalem, itself, is well over 5,000 years old and is one of the oldest, continuously inhabited areas in the world. At the time of Jesus its population was about 50,000 (just a bit smaller than Bloomington, Indiana), and this would swell to 180,000 or so (about the size of Fort Wayne, Indiana) during those times of the year when people like the Holy Family would walk to Jerusalem for the Jewish Festivals such as the Passover.

In about 1,000 B.C. King David made Jerusalem the capitol of the Israelite tribes. And David's son, King Solomon, built the First Temple of the Jews.

In 587 B.C. the Babylonians conquered Judah, where Jerusalem is located and destroyed the Temple. They took many of the Jews to Babylonia as slaves. Almost 50 years later, in 538 B.C., King Cyrus of Persia conquered Babylonia and allowed the Jews to return to Jerusalem where they then rebuilt their Temple. In 54 B.C. the Temple's treasures were stolen by the Roman General, Crassus. When Herod the Great was named King of the Jews by Rome in 37 B.C. he took control of Jerusalem and began renovating and rebuilding the Temple. Herod's Temple was the one that Jesus would have worshiped in.

In 70 A.D., following the death of Jesus, the Romans destroyed the Temple for good following another Jewish revolt. Only the Temple's western wall, now called the wailing wall, remain standing. And today the Moslem's have their beautiful Dome of the Rock built where Solomon's Temple stood. According to the Biblical Archeology Review it was built by Caliph Abd al-Malik in 691 A.D. directly over "the rock mass from which, according to Moslem tradition, Mohammed ascended to heaven. Jewish tradition views the rock as the place where Abraham nearly sacrificed Isaac (Moslems counter that it was Abraham's other son, their ancestor Ishmael, instead). Everyone agrees, however, that Jerusalem's First Temple, built by Solomon, and the Second Temple, greatly expanded by King Herod, stood somewhere on the same mount that now holds the Dome of the Rock..."

During the time of Jesus, Jerusalem was a vibrant, alive city. Here is Kathleen Ritmeyer's revealing account of that time in her short piece "A Pilgrim's Journey", courtesy of Biblical Archeology Review and the author. It does not take a great leap of faith to visualize that she could be writing about Jesus as he visits Jerusalem and the Temple Mount:

"Jerusalem is bathed in the clear light of early morning. A pilgrim has come for one of the many festivals, and his journey is almost over. He begins the ascent from the Siloam Pool at the bottom part of the Lower City. The sun is not yet casting its harsh glare on the stepped street paved with large limestone slabs, which is the path he must take to the Temple Mount. The pilgrim's eyes rest for a moment on the glittering spikes of the Temple in the distance; then he moves on. The houses of the Lower City are spread out before him like the crescent of the moon; higher up, on his left, he can see the magnificent palaces of the nobility in the Upper City. As he proceeds up the valley past the oldest part of the city, established by David and Solomon, he can still see, on his right, some of the splendid old palaces."

"All along the street the merchants of the Lower Market are busy setting up their stalls for the day's business. The pilgrim is jostled by the farmers and traders who have come to buy and sell and by their beasts of burden. Baskets of luscious fruit, piles of cheeses, jars of wine and mounds of bread are set out hurriedly on the rough wooden tables. The unloading of bales of richly colored silks from a wagon causes an outbreak of excitement and arguing."

"At the end of this stepped street, the pilgrim comes to a busy intersection. Visitors from many lands-Ethiopians, Macedonians, Cretans, Parthians and Romans from every part of the Roman empire-are moving toward the great plaza that fronts the monumental staircase leading up to the Double Gate of the Temple Mount. A different language from each group of people creates a cacophony of sound."

"Our pilgrim climbs the first flights of the imposing staircase that leads to a gate in the western wall. The hubbub of the markets becomes fainter. He reaches the central platform of the staircase, which affords him a fine view and an opportunity to rest. The whole of the Lower City and a large portion of the Upper City are spread out before him."

"On the west, the Upper City has the appearance of an impenetrable wall, the houses are so densely packed together. The Hasmonean Palace, built before Herod's time, rises high above its surroundings, and people can be seen moving about on its roof. Looking north, he sees the archives building and the Xystos, the open-air plaza where the athletic games were held during the Hellenistic period, in front of the old city wall. On the other side of the plaza, opposite the Xystos, stands the elegant Council House, or Bule, whose outer walls match the walls of the Temple Mount for beauty. A procession of priests moves solemnly over the bridge that spans the Tyropoeon Valley, a bridge that gives the priests and nobles direct access from the Upper City to the Temple Mount. The thronged street below veers off to the northwest in the direction of the city gate that leads to Damascus. As far as the eye can see, the Upper Market is crowded with milling traders, buyers and visitors attired in strange costumes."

"The pilgrim braces himself for the remaining climb up the staircase that leads to the Temple Mount. Flanked by two massive limestone pillars, so highly polished that they resemble marble, the gate evokes deep awe from the pilgrim. Looking up, he admires the gold-plated Corinthian capitals that crown the pillars. Inside the propylaeum, or gate-building, the shade is refreshing. Groups of people linger, luxuriating in the respite from glare and bustle."

"A different scene greets the eye as he enters the Royal Stoa proper on the Temple Mount. A long wall, supported by four rows of thick columns stretches out in front of him. The northern side is open and leads to the Temple court. Long shafts of dust-flecked sunlight are filtered through the windows in the upper part of the stoa and glance off a scene of frenzied commercial activity. At the tables of the moneychangers, the pilgrim exchanges coins bearing the image of Caesar for silver shekels without the forbidden graven image. Women who have recently given

110

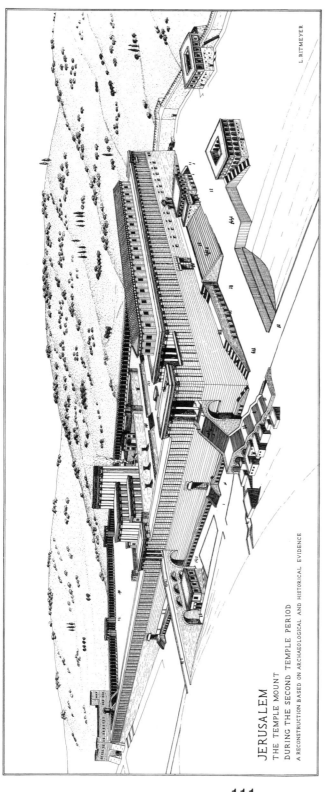

JERUSALEM
THE TEMPLE MOUNT
DURING THE SECOND TEMPLE PERIOD
A RECONSTRUCTION BASED ON ARCHAEOLOGICAL AND HISTORICAL EVIDENCE

L. RITMEYER

When King Herod rebuilt Solomon's Temple , just before the time of Jesus, he doubled the size of the original Temple Mount to the size of 24 football fields, nearly 145 acres. The original Temple had been built by King Solomon in the 10th Century B.C. and destroyed in 586 B.C. by the Babylonians. Worshippers would have entered thru numerous gates as shown. The large structure at the right was the Royal Stoa. This grand hall was also the meeting place for "the Sanhedrin-the supreme Jewish legislative, religious and judicial body," according to Ritmeyer, the world's leading authority on the Temple Mount. This was also where the money-changers were located and where the doves and other animals were sold for sacrifice in the Temple. The tall structure in the middle of the drawing was the Temple, itself, that Jesus worshiped in. It was known as the Second Temple. The structure at the far left corner was the Antonia Fortress. Jerusalem and the Temple were destroyed by the Romans in 70 A.D.

birth are crowded at the stalls nearby, haggling over the price of the doves and pigeons they will sacrifice in gratitude for the happy conclusions of their pregnancies. Those who successfully complete a purchase walk away bearing small cages. Oxen and sheep to be sacrificed are also offered for sale; the smell of their droppings permeates the entire area."

"At the eastern end of the portico is a partition through which members of the Sanhedrin are emerging after a session. The pilgrim observes on the other side of the partition the beauty of the apse, specially constructed to accommodate the Sanhedrin. A magnificent stone arch covered with a rich variety of geometric and floral patterns forms the backdrop for the Sanhedrin conferences. The tiers of smooth stone steps on which they sit while conferring are now empty."

"Leaving behind the noise of the cooing doves and the bleating animals, the pilgrim moves on and passes through the open portico in the direction of the Temple. Soon, merging with the crowds pouring out of the underground stairway leading up from the Double Gate, he becomes part of the great throng who have come to worship at the 'House of the Lord'."

Mrs. Ritmeyer's husband, Dr. Leen Ritmeyer, a Dutchman who lived in Jerusalem for 16 of his 22 years in Israel, has done a great deal of work locating the actual site of the Temple, and has even nailed down where the Ark of the Covenant sat in the Holy of Holies. The Ritmeyers met in the 1970's while both were working in the archeological dig just south of the Temple Mount. Their small book "Secrets of Jerusalem's Temple Mount" is filled with drawings and photos of the area.

Edersheim completes the picture of the Temple's dominant effect on the city when he writes-"Each morning the threefold blast of the priest's trumpets wakened the city with a call to prayer; each evening the same blasts closed the working day, as with sounds from heaven. Turn where you might, everywhere the holy buildings were in view, now with the smoke of sacrifices curling over the courts, or again with solemn stillness resting upon the sacred halls. It was the Temple which gave its character to Jerusalem, and which decided its fate."

And Daniel-Rops writes of the odors and the noise of the city-"The whole city, more or less, was filled with a strong smell, made up of many elements. There was a police regulation forbidding 'open-air ovens, because of the smoke' and another which forbade the use of manure for trees and flowers. But the existence

of these regulations was surprising, for the smell of the hot grease of cooking mingled with the sharp stench of rubbish that, according to the Talmud, was swept
away from the open places every day, but which was no doubt scarcely ever disturbed in the alleys. Furthermore, if the wind blew from the east only a little, the
smoke from the altar of sacrifices would turn back not only into the courts but over
the whole city, bringing a mixture of the horrible reek of burning flesh and the
heady smell of incense. The Jewish crowd had a reputation of smelling unpleas-
ant, and indeed this was one of the stock jokes of Roman heavy comedy; yet the
women used a great deal of scent, and it was said that they went to great
extremes to surround themselves with a sensuous perfume when they thought this
was called for. In vain the rabbis said, 'The incense of the Temple ought to be
enough for you.' The upper market, where myrrh and nard and costly balm were
sold, was always crowded."

"The town was not only rich in odors; it was also rich in noise. Except at night
and during the very hot hours of the siesta or in winter when the west wind
brought its piercing blasts of rain, the whole city was filled with a confused din.
Everything was mingled to form this general sound: the shouting of the tradesmen
trying to attract customers, the cry of the water-carriers bearing their skins on their
backs and offering their services, the public criers who called for silence to make
an official announcement, and sometimes the shouting of the guards making way
for some condemned man who was being taken to 'the place of the skull,' carrying
the beam of his cross upon his back. The animals being driven toward the Temple
bleated and lowed; sometimes the asses brayed, but more rarely, since they had
learned patience. A group of pilgrims would pass, singing a psalm in chorus to the
tune of The Doe of the Morning or The Dove of the Faraway Terebinths. In the
fullers quarter might be heard the dull, monotonous noise of fulling; in the quarter
of the coppersmiths, the rhythmic din of hammering. And then, four times a day, at
the hour of sacrifice and at the three ritual pauses, the triple blast of the seven silver trumpets rang out from the gate of the men's court in the Temple and imposed
a comparative silence, during which the pious prostrated themselves."

There is a great deal of information and speculation available from Biblical
Archeology Review articles over the years on what the Temple Mount and the
actual Temple itself looked like. The historian of that day, Josephus, says that "the
level area on the summit of the Temple hill was originally barely large enough for
shrine and altar, but was gradually enlarged by additions to the embankment
through the ages." BAR says that "today the outside measurements of the Temple

area are reckoned at 912 feet on the south side, 1,035 feet on the north, 1,536 feet on the east, and 1, 590 feet on the west. The level of the courtyard is 2,418 feet above sea level, and the total area is some thirty-five acres."

In "The Archeology of the New Testament" the Biblical Archeology Review team gives this fascinating description of the Temple area and actual Temple, itself, that Jesus would have walked and worshiped in:

"Entry into the Temple area was by gates on all four sides...Within the Temple area and evidently running around it on all sides were great "stoas" or porticoes which, Josephus says, were reconstructed by Herod from the foundations. For the most part these consisted of double rows of monolithic marble columns, twenty-five cubits high, with ceilings of cedar panels. On the south side the colonnade known as the Royal Portico was more elaborate still. On the east side the colonnade bore the name of Solomon. These porticoes enclosed the 'first court', and this large area was entirely paved with varicolored stones. The court was freely open even to Gentiles, but at the edge of the next court a stone balustrade three cubits high carried slabs giving warning, some in Greek and some in Latin, that no foreigner might go farther under threat of penalty of death."

One of these stone slabs with a complete inscription in Greek was found by Clermont-Ganneau and published in l871. The text reads: "No foreigner is to enter within the balustrade and enclosure around the temple area. Whoever is caught will have himself to blame for his death which will follow."

"The 'second court' beyond this balustrade was a quadrangular area screened by a wall of its own, forty cubits in height. Fourteen steps led up to a terrace around the wall and five more steps ascended to the gates in the wall. The first part of this entire second court was walled off to make a special place into which all Jewish women, whether natives of the country or visitors from abroad, were allowed to go. Access was through a gate on the north side, a gate on the south, and a gate on the east. Opposite the last gate another gate allowed access to the second part of the second court, namely, the part into which only Israelite men might go, for which there were also three gates on the north side and three gates on the south. Of the ten gates now accounted for, nine were overlaid with gold and silver, but one was of Corinthian bronze and far exceeded in value the ones that were plated with silver and set in gold...Still farther within was the 'third court', which only the priests were allowed to enter. Here was the great altar (standing, we think, on the sacred rock) on which whole burnt-offerings were sacrificed. Behind it to the west, and approached by its own flight of twelve steps, was the temple edifice proper. The facade of its porch was of equal height and breadth, each being 100 cubits. The interior of the building itself was 60 cubits high, 60 cubits long, and 20 cubits wide. The first room, 40 cubits long, contained the seven-armed lampstand, the table for the bread of presence, and the altar of incense...The second room of the temple edifice was 20 cubits long and screened from the first room by a veil. In it was no furniture whatsoever. 'Unapproachable, inviolable, invisible to all, it was called the Holy of Holy'."

Today, Jerusalem is a city of three Sabbaths. Friday belongs to the Moslems, Saturday to the Jews, and Sunday to the Christians. And all three religions revere the Temple Mount.

Sources for this chapter, and recommended reading for you:

Henri Daniel-Rops, Daily Life in the Time of Jesus, An authentic reconstruction of Biblical Palestine and the day-to-day lives and customs of its people. © 1962 Hawthorn Books, Inc. 70 Fifth Avenue, New York, NY 10011. Mentor-Omega Book Edition, Published by The New American Library. Originally published in France by Librairie Hachette, © 1961.

Dr. Leen Ritmeyer, The Ark of the Covenant, Where It Stood in Solomon's Temple. Biblical Archeology Review, January/February 1996. Pages 46-55, 70-72.

Dr. Leen Ritmeyer, Locating the Original Temple Mount. Biblical Archeology Review, March/April 1992. Pages 24-45.

Dr. Leen and Kathleen Ritmeyer, Secrets of Jerusalem's Temple Mount. © 1998, Biblical Archeology Review. Foreword by Hershel Shanks, Editor, Biblical Archeology Review.

Dr. Alfred Edersheim, Sketches of Jewish Social Life, in the days of Christ. Wm. B. Eerdmans Publishing Company, Grand Rapids, Michigan.

Dr. Alfred Edersheim, The Life And Times of Jesus The Messiah. Wm. B. Eerdmans Publishing Company, Grand Rapids, Michigan.

Readers Digest, Atlas of the Bible, An Illustrated Guide to the Holy Land. ©
1981, The Reader's Digest Association, Inc.

Jack Finegan, The Archeology of the New Testament, The Life of Jesus and
the Beginning of the Early Church. © 1992 by Princeton University Press.
Published by Princeton University Press, 41 William Street, Princeton, NJ 08540.

Hershel Shanks & Dan P. Cole, Edited by, Archaeology and the Bible, The
Best of BAR. Archaeology in the World of Herod, Jesus and Paul, Volume Two. ©
1990 Biblical Archaeology Society, 3000 Connecticut Avenue, N.W., Washington,
D.C. 20008.

His Crucifixion

This is such a well-known story that it seems impossible that there could be anything new to add to it. However, a medical doctor by the name of C. Truman Davis wrote a fascinating article a few years ago for Arizona Medicine from a physician's point-of-view that contains some very interesting insight into the physical suffering and death of Yeshua bar Yosef (Jesus Christ). Excerpts follow.

Dr. Davis tells us that the Persians were the first to have practiced killing people by crucifixion. At the time of the Romans the person condemned to death was forced to carry to the place of execution his own crossbeam (the patibulum) that weighed about 110 pounds. The vertical post (the stipes) was permanently anchored into the ground atop a skull-shaped hill.

In addition, most artists have shown the nails driven into the palms of the hands of the person being crucified; however, Dr. Davis reveals that this is erroneous and if this had been done the nails would have stripped out between the fingers and could not have supported the weight of the body. Instead, he says Roman historical accounts indicate that the nails were actually driven between the small bones of the wrists. He says that the wrists have anatomically always been considered part of the hands, and therefore, when Jesus tells Thomas to "Observe my hands" it would also have referred to his wrists.

We all know that Pontius Pilate condemned Jesus to scourging and crucifixion. Scourging was done by stripping the person of their clothing and tying their arms to a post above their heads. They were then beaten at least 40 times with a short whip (the flagellum) consisting of heavy, leather strips with small lead balls attached to their ends. Dr. Davis tells us that these would have first cut through the skin and then deeper into the subcutaneous tissues until the skin of the back is "hanging in long ribbons and the entire area is an unrecognizable mass of torn bleeding tissue."

The Roman soldiers then made the crown of thorns out of branches commonly used for firewood and forced it down upon his head. This would have caused heavy bleeding since the head is one of the most vascular parts of the body.

In this painful, weakened, suffering state, Jesus was then forced to carry the crossbeam from prison up to Calvary along the Via Dolorosa. According to Dr. Davis this would have been about a 650 yard distance from the fortress Antonia to Golgotha. We know from the Bible that a North African, Simon of Cyrene, helped Jesus carry his burden. Once there, Jesus is cruelly thrown to the ground with his ravaged back against the coarse wooden beam and the "heavy, square, wrought-iron" nails are driven through his wrists and into the wood. The patibulum is then lifted, with Jesus attached, onto the top of the vertical beam and the placard, "Jesus of Nazareth, King of the Jews" is nailed above his head. The Gospel according to St. John tells us that this was written in Hebrew, Greek and Latin.

Dr. Davis then tells us that "the left foot is pressed backward against the right foot, and with both feet extended, toes down, a nail is driven through the arch of each, leaving the knees moderately flexed. The victim is now crucified. As he slowly sags down with more weight upon the nails in the wrists, excruciating, fiery pain shoots along the fingers and up the arms to explode in the brain—the nails in the wrists are putting pressure on the median nerves. As he pushes himself upward to avoid this wrenching torment, he places his full weight on the nail through his feet. Again there is the searing agony of the tearing through the nerves between the metatarsal bones of the feet."

"At this point, another phenomenon occurs. As the arms fatigue, great waves of cramps sweep over the muscles, knotting them in deep, relentless, throbbing pain. With these cramps comes the inability to push himself upward. Hanging by his arms, the pectoral muscles are paralyzed and the intercostal muscles are unable to act. Air can be drawn into the lungs, but cannot be exhaled. Jesus fights to raise himself in order to get even one short breath. Finally carbon dioxide builds up in the lungs and the blood stream and the cramps partially subside. Spasmodically, he is able to push Himself upward to exhale and bring in the life-giving oxygen. It was undoubtedly during these periods that he uttered the seven short sentences which are recorded:

Regarding the Roman soldiers - "Father, forgive them for they know not what they do."

To the penitent thief hanging beside him - "Today thou shalt be with me in Paradise."

To his beloved Apostle, John - "Behold thy mother" and then to Mary, his mother - "Woman, behold thy son."

The fourth cry is from the beginning of the 22nd Psalm - "My God, my God, why hast thou forsaken me?"

Dr. Davis says that "hours of this limitless pain, cycles of twisting joint-rending cramps, intermittent partial asphyxiation, searing pain as tissue is torn from his lacerated back as he moves up and down against the rough timber. Then another agony begins. A deep crushing pain deep in the chest as the pericardium slowly fills with serum and begins to compress the heart."

According to Dr. Davis "It is now almost over—the loss of tissue fluids has reached a critical level—the compressed heart is struggling to pump heavy, thick sluggish blood into the tissue—the tortured lungs are making a frantic effort to draw in small gulps of air. The markedly dehydrated tissues send their flood of stimuli to the brain."

Jesus gasps his fifth cry - "I thirst!"

"A sponge soaked in Posca, the cheap, sour wine which is the staple drink of the Roman legionnaires, is lifted to His lips. He apparently does not take any of the liquid. The body of Jesus is now in extremis, and he can feel the chill of death creeping through his tissues. This realization brings out his sixth words—possibly little more than a tortured whisper:

"It is finished."

"His mission of atonement has now been completed. Finally he can allow his body to die."

"With one last surge of strength, he once again presses his torn feet against the nail, straightens his legs, takes a deeper breath, and utters his seventh and last cry, "Father into thy hands I commit my spirit."

"Apparently to make doubly sure of death, the legionnaire drove his lance through the fifth interspace between the ribs, upward through the pericardium and into the heart. The 34th verse of the 19th chapter of the Gospel according to John:

'And immediately there came out blood and water.' Thus there was an escape of watery fluid from the sac surrounding the heart and blood from the interior of the heart. We, therefore, have rather conclusive postmortem evidence that Our Lord died, not the usual crucifixion death by suffocation, but of heart failure due to shock and constriction of the heart by fluid in the pericardium."

And, of course, this deeply depressing account is wiped away when we read the story of Easter morning!

He has risen from the dead!

Sources for this chapter, and recommended reading for you:

Dr. C. Truman Davis, The Crucifixion of Jesus, The Passion of Christ from a Medical Point of View.   Arizona Medicine Magazine, March, 1965.

Hershel Shanks, New Analysis of the Crucified Man. Biblical Archaeology Review, November/December 1985, Vol. XI, No. 6. Pages 20-21.

Henri Daniel-Rops, Daily Life in the Time of Jesus, An authentic reconstruction of Biblical Palestine and the day-to-day lives and customs of its people. © 1962 Hawthorn Books, Inc. 70 Fifth Avenue, New York, NY 10011. Mentor-Omega Book Edition, Published by The New American Library. Originally published in France by Librairie Hachette, © 1961.

Dr.Alfred Edersheim, The Life And Times of Jesus The Messiah. Wm. B. Eerdmans Publishing Company, Grand Rapids, Michigan.

Giuseppe Ricciotti, University of Rome, The Life of Christ. Translated by Alba I. Zizzamia, Trinity College, Washington, D.C. © 1947 The Bruce Publishing Company, Milwaukee, Wisconsin. Imprimatur Michael J. Curley, D.D., Archbishop of Baltimore and Washington.

Doubleday & Company, Inc. Great Events of Bible Times, New Perspecitves on the People, Places, and History of the Biblical World. ©1987 by Marshall Editions Limited, 170 Piccadilly, London W1V 9DD England. Published in the United States by Doubleday & Company, Inc., 666 Fifth Avenue, New York, NY 10103

The Rest of His Story

This chapter is not mine to write. It can be found in the five Gospels of Matthew, Mark, Luke, John, and Acts, and in the two thousand years of recorded history written after his death...in the deeds and words of those who have worshiped and questioned him since as the God-Man/Son of God.

Albert Nolan, in his book "Jesus before Christianity" says that "The four small books that we call the gospels are not biographies and were never intended to be. Their purpose was to show how Jesus could be relevant to people who lived outside Palestine a generation or two after Jesus' death. This first generation of Christians obviously did not feel the need for an exact biography of Jesus' life. They wanted to know how Jesus might be relevant to them in their situation outside Palestine."

You can read of his Ministry in the Gospels, as well as of his Trial, Death and Resurrection. My purpose in this small book has been to fill in the blanks about some of the other things that I have always wondered about Jesus and his everyday life. I hope we both have a better understanding of him and his times as a result.

It has been a mitzvah writing this book. May it have been one for you in the reading.

God Bless!

And God forgives!

Sources for this chapter, and recommended reading for you:

Rev. Albert Nolan, JESUS, Before Christianity. © 1976 by Albert Nolan. Published in the U.S. by Orbis Books, Maryknoll, New York 10545.

Author Profiles

As I stated at the beginning of this book, I did not make any of this up. It was gleaned from the arduous work and writings of many learned men and women. I was simply a beachcomber meandering along through all they have written and done, selecting those breathtaking seashells of fact and conjecture that I thought would help tell the story of Jesus, Mary and Joseph and their times. I have tried to be as faithful as I could about attributing their work to them by using quotation marks. If I have erred in any cases in doing so, it was purely unintentional given the volume of research and note-taking that went into putting this book together over a period of about 10 years. Here is a bit more about who these extraordinary people are that I have quoted from, or referenced, from the author's notes accompanying their works and from other sources. In alphabetical order:

Nahman Avigad - Author of the Biblical Archaeology Review article "Jerusalem Flourishing-A Craft Center for Stone, Pottery, and Glass". The eminent Israeli archaeologist, Avigad grew up in Austria and Czechoslovakia. In 1925 he immigrated to Israel, attended Hebrew University in Jerusalem and joined its faculty in 1949. He held degrees in archaeology, architecture and philosophy. Led important excavations, not only in the Upper City of Jerusalem, but also in the Judean Desert Caves, Beth She'arim and Masada.

Dr. Richard Batey - Author of "Jesus & the Forgotten City". He served as administrative director of the University of South Florida's excavations at Sepphoris from 1982 to 1983 and was assistant director from 1984 to 1989. He is the W. J. Millard Professor of Religion at Rhodes College and also the author of "Jesus and the Poor". His Ph.D. degree is from Vanderbilt University.

Professor E.M. Blaiklock - Author of "Today's Handbook of Bible Characters". Emeritus Professor of Classics at Auckland University in New Zealand for over twenty-one years. Internationally known as a writer on classical and biblical subjects. A consulting editor to the New International Version of the Holy Bible.

Jane Cahill et al - With Karl Reinhard, David Tarler and Peter Warnock she authored the Biblical Archaeology Review article "It Had to Happen-Scientists Examine Contents of Ancient Bathroom". Cahill and Tarler are senior staff members at the City of David excavations. They have also co-directed the excavation of Tell el-Hammah in the Jordan Valley. Reinhard is professor of biological anthropology at the University of Nebraska at Lincoln. At the time of this work, Warnock was a graduate student at Texas A&M University studying botanical remains. He had worked on the pollen, seeds, and wood charcoal from a number of sites in Israel and Jordan.

Henri Daniel-Rops - Author of "Daily Life in the Time of Jesus". This is the nom de plume of Henri Jules Charles Petiot, born in 1901 in France. He was a Professor of History until his retirement in 1945 at Neuilly. He wrote more than 70 books under this name and received many honors, including Commander of the Order of Saint Gregory the Great from Pope Pius XII and the Grand Cross, conferred by Pope John XXIII. His best-known books in this country are "This is the Mass" and "Jesus and His Times". He also served as editor-in-chief of "The Twentieth Century Encyclopedia of Catholicism", a 150-volume work.

C. Truman Davis, M.D. - Author of "The Crucifixion of Jesus, The Passion of Christ from a Medical Point of View." Reprinted from the March, 1965 issue of Arizona Medicine.

Rabbi Hayim Halevy Donin - Author of "To Pray As A Jew". For twenty years he was Rabbi of Congregation B'nai David in Southfield, Michigan where he was also Adjunct Professor of Judaic Studies at the University of Detroit. Held a Ph.D. in Education.

Dr. Alfred Edersheim - Author of "The Life and Times of Jesus The Messiah", the most extensively used life of Christ in the English language, and "Sketches of Jewish Social Life in the Days of Christ". Was of Jewish extraction, born in Vienna in 1825. Converted to Christianity, he studied theology at New College, Edinburgh, Scotland and the University of Berlin. Became a clergyman in the Church of England and served as Grinfield Lecturer in the University of Oxford from 1884 to 1889, the year of his death.

Dr. Stephen Fine - Author, with Ann Killebrew of the Biblical Archaeology Review article "Qatzrin-Reconstructing Village Life in Talmudic Times". At the time the article was written he was a doctoral candidate at Hebrew University, in the department of Jewish History, and a visiting lecturer in the University's Rothberg School for Overseas Students.

Rev. Joseph A. Fitzmyer - Author of the Biblical Archaeology Review article "Did Jesus Speak Greek?". A Jesuit priest, Fitzmyer is professor emeritus of Biblical Studies at Catholic University of America in Washington, D.C. and is a past president of the Society of Biblical Literature and of the Catholic Biblical Association. One of the world's leading Dead Sea Scroll scholars.

Rabbi Louis Jacobs - Author of the "Concise Companion to the Jewish Religion". Rabbi of the New London Synagogue and Goldsmid Visiting Professor at University College London. He is the author of many books and hundreds of learned articles on Judaism, Talmud, Jewish Mysticism, and general Jewish thought.

Dr. Ann Killebrew - Author with Dr. Stephen Fine of the Biblical Archaeology Review article "Qatzrin-Reconstructing Village Life In Talmudic Times". She spent nine-years working at this ancient Golan village site. She has been a lecturer in the Foreign Students Program at Hebrew University in Jerusalem and has also served as a research fellow at the W.F. Albright Institute of Archaeological Research. Her field experience also includes work at Tel Akko, Tel Miqne, Tel Beth-Shean and Tel Gezer.

Professor John C.H. Laughlin - Author of the Biblical Archaeology Review article "Capernaum, From Jesus' Time and After". A popular lecturer at BAR seminars, Laughlin is professor of religion at Averett College in Danville, Virginia. In addition to Capernaum, he has excavated at Ten Dan and Banias (Caesarea Philippi).

Eugene J. Lipman - Author of "The Mishnah-Oral Teachings of Judaism".

Professor Steve Mason - Author of the Biblical Archaeology Review article "Will the Real Josephus Please Stand Up?". He is associate professor of classics and religious studies at York University in Ontario. He has written two books on Josephus and has recently been commissioned to prepare a new English translation of Josephus' works.

Dr. John McRay - Author of the description of the services in the synagogue during the time of Jesus on ChristianityOnline.com. Professor of New Testament and Archaeology at Wheaton College Graduate School. Also the author of "Archaeology and the New Testament". Supervised excavating teams at Sepphoris, Caesarea Maritima and Herodium. Has served as archaeological consultant to National Geographic Magazine, A&E Television Channel, Reader's Digest and others. Worldwide lecturer at colleges and universities in Australia, England, Russia, etc.

Rev. John P. Meier - Author of "A Marginal Jew, Rethinking The Historical Jesus". A Catholic priest, Father Meier is professor of the New Testament at the Catholic University of America in Washington, D.C. and has been both the president of the Catholic Biblical Association and the general editor of the Catholic Biblical Quarterly.

Dr. John W. Miller - Author of "Jesus At Thirty". Holds the Th.D. from the University of Basel and is Professor Emeritus of Religious Studies at Conrad Grebel College, University of Waterloo, Ontario. He was cofounder and cochair of the Historical Jesus Section in the Society of Biblical Literature.

Professor Jacob Neusner - Author of "Judaism in the Beginning of Christianity". Professor at Brown University and the author of many learned books, including the ground-breaking trilogy "The Foundations of Judaism: Method, Teleology, Doctrine".

Mendall Nun - Author of two Biblical Archaeology Review articles referenced in this book-"Cast Your Net Upon the Waters. Fish and Fishermen in Jesus' Time" and "Ports of Galilee, Modern Drought Reveals Harbors from Jesus' Time". Born in Latvia, Nun immigrated to Palestine in 1939. Two years later he joined Kibbutz Ein Gev, on the eastern shore of the Sea of Galilee, where he worked as a fisherman. Nun (his name means "fish" in Aramaic) has become the area's resident expert on the history of the Sea of Galilee and its fishing trade. He received the Ben-Zvi prize in 1964 for his book "Ancient Jewish Fisheries".

Dr. Wolfgang E. Pax - Author of the book "In The Footsteps of Jesus". Pax is the director of the Institute for Bible Research on the Via Dolorosa in the Old City of Jerusalem. He earned a Ph.D. in Semitic languages at the University of Breslau.

C.M. Pelkington - Author of "Judaism" in the Teach Yourself Series, he is a lecturer in religious studies and the author of school textbooks on Judaism.

Kathleen Ritmeyer - Author of "A Pilgrim's Journey" in "Secrets of Jerusalem's Temple Mount". Archaeological researcher and writer. Married to Leen Ritmeyer, who she met while working on the Temple Mount project. Ritmeyer has also taken part in excavations in Tel Akko in Israel, in the Outer Hebrides in Scotland and in the west of her native Ireland.

Dr. Leen Ritmeyer - Author of "Secrets of Jerusalem's Temple Mount". Has worked as an archaeological architect on Jerusalem's major digs, including the Temple Mount, the Jewish Quarter, the Citadel and the City of David. Ph.D. in archaeology from the University of Manchester, England. Served as architect of the Temple Mount excavation in Jerusalem from 1973-78. He is the world's leading expert on the archaeology of the Temple Mount. Married to Kathleen Ritmeyer, whom he met during that Temple Mount work.

Dr. C. Bernard Ruffin - Author of "The Twelve, The Lives of the Apostles After Calvary". Also the author of Padre Pio: The True Story, Dr. Ruffin has written many articles on Gospel harmony and was most recently a member of the Executive Board of the Hymn Society of America.

Professor Anthony J. Saldarini - Author of the Biblical Archaeology Review article "Babatha's Story. Personal Archive Offers a Glimpse of Ancient Jewish Life". Professor in the department of theology at Boston College, he has written extensively on Judaism in the Greco-Roman period and is book review editor for Bible Review Magazine, the sister publication to Biblical Archaeology Review.

Hershel Shanks - Author with James F. Strange of the Biblical Archaeology Review article "Synagogue Where Jesus Preached Found at Capernaum". Shanks is the Editor of the Biblical Archaeology Review and Bible Review, and a leading writer on the Dead Sea Scrolls. He is an expert on the history and archaeology of ancient synagogues.

Rabbi Milton Steinberg - Author of "Basic Judaism". Graduated from City College of New York and was awarded a master's degree in philosophy by Columbia University. The recipient of an honorary degree of Doctor of Hebrew Letters from the Jewish Theological Seminary of America, he was Rabbi of the Park Avenue Synagogue in New York until his death.

Professor James F. Strange - Author with Hershel Shanks of the Biblical Archaeology Review articles "Synagogue Where Jesus Preached Found at Capernaum" and "Has the House Where Jesus Stayed in Capernaum Been Found?" Strange is Dean of the College of Arts and Letters at the University of South Florida and professor in the university's Department of Religious Studies, and has directed the university's excavations in Lower Galilee since 1983.

Shelley Wachsmann - Author of the Biblical Archaeology Review article "The Galilee Boat. 2,000-Year-Old Hull Recovered Intact". Nautical archaeologist for the Israel Antiquities Authority, responsible for discovering, recording and protecting Israel's nautical heritage.

Rabbi Stephen M. Weylan - Author of "The Jews in the Time of Jesus". Rabbi at Temple Beth Tikvah, Wayne, New Jersey. Also the author of "Settings of Silver".

Professor Irving Zeitlin - Author of "Jesus and the Judaism of His Time". Professor of Sociology at the University of Toronto.

Related Websites
(The author and publisher assumes no responsibility for these websites, these are only being published as a convenience for our readers.)

www.christianity.com
www.christusrex.org/www1/pater/JPN-aramaic.html
http://mahal.zrc.ac.il/ancient-boat/bot-link.htm
www.stolaf.edu/people/kchanson/fishing.html
www.israel-mfa.gov.il/facts/hist/arcsit3.html
www.furman.edu/~mcknight/galreg9.htm
www.ginosar.co.il/center.htm
www.infotour.co.il/itm_opt.cgi?5516+42
www.bib-arch.org

The Jesus Digest

**What you never knew about the everyday life of Jesus.
Learn what it was like to live when he did.**

By Dick Lattimer

Pick up additional copies where you purchased this copy of "The Jesus Digest,"© for family or friends, or send $14.95, plus $3.00 shipping and handling to:

The Whispering Eagle Press, Inc.
P.O. Box 344
Cedar Key, Florida 32625

Florida residents add 6% sales tax.

If your church or youth group would like to use "The Jesus Digest"© to raise money for your various projects, please write to us on your church stationary and we will give you a quote on your bulk cost for such fundraising activities. Tell us about how many you would like to order.